NOVEL METHODS OF TEACHING

FOCUS ON NEP-2020

Mrs. Neetu Sharda

Dr. Rajpal Kosaliya

Mr. Suryakant Swami

Mr. Anil Kumar Grewal

Dr. Naveen Kumar

Title   : Novel Method of Teaching

Author   : Mrs. Neetu Sharda, Dr. Rajpal Kosaliya, Mr. Suryakant Swami,
           Mr. Anil Kumar Grewal, Dr. Naveen Kumar

Edition : First (December, 2024)

ISBN   : 9789348332080

Published by

PRACHI
DIGITAL PUBLICATION

Regd. Add.: 254, Khuriyakhatta No. 10, Bindukhatta,
Lalkuan, Nainital - 262402, Uttarakhand, India
Website : www.prachidigital.com
E-mail : info@prachidigital.in
Phone : +91 976041 7980, +91 976041 8103

Printed by :

Manipal Technologies Limited, Bengaluru - 560001, Karnataka

PREFACE

In an era marked by rapid technological advancement and globalization, the field of education is undergoing a transformative revolution. The National Education Policy (NEP) 2020 stands at the forefront of this change, advocating for a comprehensive reimagining of teaching and learning methodologies in India. This book, "Novel Methods of Teaching in India: Focus on NEP-2020," aims to explore and elucidate the innovative pedagogical strategies that are reshaping Indian classrooms, preparing educators and students alike for the challenges of the 21st century. The evolution of education in India has been a journey through rich historical contexts, cultural paradigms, and socio-economic dynamics. Yet, as we step into a future driven by knowledge and skills, it becomes imperative to move away from traditional, rote-based learning models toward more interactive, student-centered approaches. This manuscript is a response to this need, offering educators, policymakers, and stakeholders a complete guide to understanding and implementing novel teaching methods that promote critical thinking, creativity, and holistic development. Throughout the chapters, we delve into various innovative teaching methodologies, such as active learning, differentiated instruction, and technology-enhanced education. Each chapter presents not only theoretical insights but also practical applications, real-world examples, and case studies from diverse educational settings across India. By showcasing successful implementations, we aim to inspire and empower educators to embrace these methods, adapting them to the unique contexts of their classrooms. Furthermore, this book addresses the challenges of implementing novel methods, highlighting the disparities in resources, infrastructure, and training that exist between urban and rural educational institutions. It emphasizes the role of teachers as facilitators of change and advocates for constant professional growth to equip instructors with the skills needed to thrive in a modern educational landscape.

We hope that this book serves as a valuable resource in your educational endeavors, guiding you toward the implementation of innovative teaching methods that will enrich the learning experiences of students across India.

Authors

CONTENTS

CHAPTER 1

INTRODUCTION TO MODERN TEACHING

1.1 The Evolution of Education in India

Education in India has experienced a significant evolution, deeply rooted in its ancient heritage, influenced by colonial legacies, and shaped by contemporary educational reforms. The transition from traditional informal education to a formal educational structure mirrors the broader socio-political and cultural transitions of the nation. Initially, Indian education was intertwined with religious teachings and spiritual development. The Gurukul system, prevalent in ancient India, centered around a guru who imparted knowledge in various fields such as philosophy, mathematics, and science to his disciples. This system emphasized a holistic educational experience, nurturing not only intellectual prowess but also ethical values and spiritual growth within a closely-knit community. However, this form of education was predominantly available to the upper echelons of society, often excluding the lower strata from its benefits.

The landscape of education began to transform with the dissemination of Buddhist and Jain philosophies, which introduced a more formalized approach to learning. Ancient universities such as Nalanda and Takshashila became beacons of learning, attracting scholars globally and marking India as a formidable center of scholarly activity. These institutions focused on a curriculum that included subjects like logic, grammar, philosophy, and medicine, establishing a foundation for India's rich academic heritage.

The British colonization of India marked another significant shift in the educational framework. The colonizers implemented a Western-style educational system, prioritizing English and designed to cultivate a workforce of clerks and administrative officials to support the British administrative machinery. This system introduced more structured educational institutions that followed a rigid curriculum but simultaneously marginalized indigenous knowledge systems and favored an examination-focused approach. While it extended educational opportunities more broadly across Indian society, it also exacerbated disparities between urban and rural populations and perpetuated existing social hierarchies by restricting access to high-quality education.

Following independence, the Indian government recognized the transformative power of education in nation-building. It undertook extensive measures to broaden educational access, including initiatives like the Right to Education Act (2009), which guarantees free and compulsory education to children between the ages of 6 and 14, thereby enshrining education as a fundamental right for all citizens. The establishment of prestigious institutions such as the Indian Institutes of Technology (IITs) and Indian Institutes of Management (IIMs) underscores India's commitment to excellence in higher education (Figure 1.1).

In recent developments, the National Education Policy (NEP) 2020 marks a progressive shift towards a flexible and interdisciplinary educational model. The NEP promotes a holistic learning paradigm that eschews rote learning in favor of fostering critical thinking, creativity, and problem-solving skills. It advocates for experiential and skill-based learning, aimed at producing individuals who are well-prepared to succeed in both local and global arenas. Furthermore, the NEP 2020 emphasizes the role of digital technologies in education, recognizing their potential to enhance accessibility and engagement, particularly in remote and underserved communities.

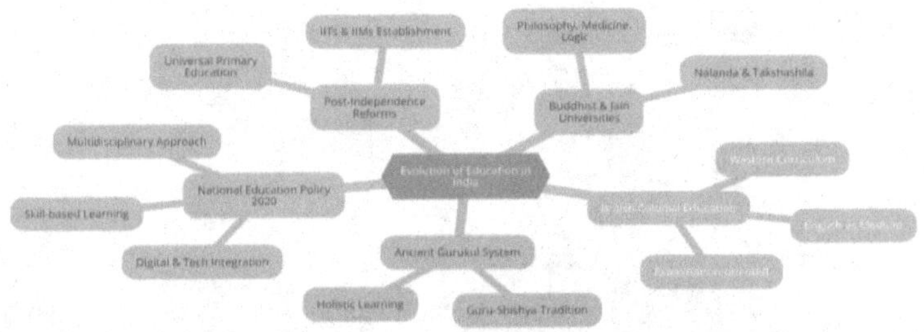

Figure 1.1: This mind map illustrates the key stages in the evolution of Indian education:

- **Ancient Gurukul System**: Focused on holistic knowledge and the traditional Guru-Shishya model.
- **Buddhist & Jain Universities**: Institutionalized education, emphasizing philosophy, medicine, and logic.
- **British Colonial Education**: Shifted to a Western curriculum, emphasizing exams and English as the medium of teaching.
- **Post-Independence Reforms**: Introduced universal primary education and established IITs & IIMs for higher education.
- **National Education Policy 2020**: Advocated a multidisciplinary approach, skill-based learning, and digital integration.

Furthermore, the NEP 2020 aims to reconcile traditional educational practices with contemporary needs by promoting the integration of indigenous knowledge, regional languages, and cultural heritage into the academic curriculum. This initiative is particularly significant in preserving India's rich heritage while simultaneously preparing students for the encounters of the 21st century.

1.2 Traditional vs. Modern Methods of Teaching in Indian Schools

Teaching methodologies in India have significantly transformed, transitioning from traditional, teacher-centric models to more modern, learner-centered approaches. This evolution is indicative of broader societal and educational shifts, taking cues from global educational trends while addressing the specific requirements of India's diverse student body. Exploring the distinctions between conventional and contemporary teaching practices sheds light on their respective advantages and shortcomings, underscoring the necessity to adapt to the current educational landscape. This adaptation is crucial in preparing students to meet the challenges of a rapidly changing world, ensuring they are not only recipients of knowledge but active participants in their learning journey.

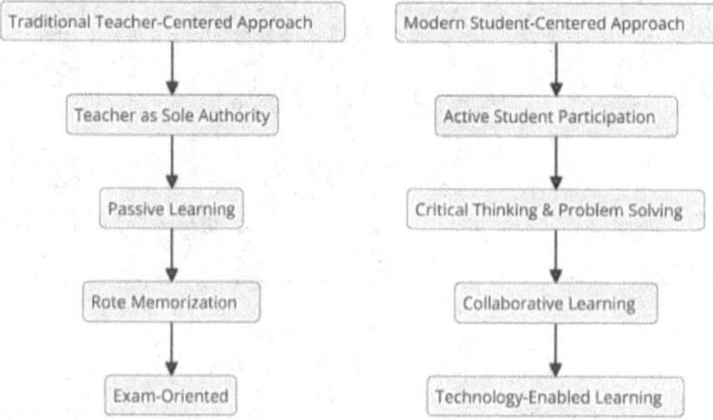

Figure 1.2: This flowchart compares traditional teacher-centered approaches with modern student-centered methods in Indian schools:

- **Traditional Teacher-Centered Approach**:
  o Teacher is the sole authority.
  o Learning is passive, focused on rote memorization.
  o Emphasizes exams and marks.
- **Modern Student-Centered Approach**:
  o Students actively participate in learning.
  o Focuses on critical thinking and problem-solving.
  o Learning is collaborative and enhanced by technology.

In the traditional educational framework of India, the teacher was the central figure in the classroom, wielding considerable authority. Education primarily followed the guru-shishya (teacher-student) paradigm, where knowledge was disseminated through lectures and rote memorization. This approach placed a strong emphasis on discipline, respect for authority, and repetitive learning to achieve mastery. Teachers served as the sole custodians of knowledge, with students expected to passively assimilate information. The curriculum, often steeped in religious, moral, or philosophical content, was strictly structured, offering limited scope for creative or exploratory activities. While this method cultivated a deep reverence for education and aided in the retention of fundamental knowledge, it significantly constrained the development of critical thinking, creativity, and innovative abilities (Figure 1.2).

In stark contrast, contemporary teaching methodologies advocate for a dynamic and learner-centric environment. Modern classrooms are designed to encourage active student participation, fostering skills such as critical thinking, problem-solving, and collaborative learning, which are indispensable in the 21st-century global landscape. Rather than mere memorization, students are encouraged to interact with the content, pose questions, and delve deeper into subjects. The role of the teacher has evolved from an authoritarian figure to a facilitator or mentor, guiding students in their exploration of information and fostering a culture of independent learning. A significant shift in modern education is the integration of technology in teaching. Tools like smartboards, tablets, and various e-learning platforms have revolutionized educational delivery and engagement.

Technological advancements provide students access to a vast array of online resources, making learning a more interactive and personalized experience. For example, students can progress at their own pace, revisit complex topics, and access additional materials for enhanced comprehension. Technology also facilitates collaborative learning, enabling students to work on joint projects and assignments remotely. The National Education Policy (NEP) 2020 supports this shift towards innovative and engaging educational practices. It champions experiential and skill-based learning, encouraging students to engage with real-world challenges and apply their learning in practical contexts. The NEP 2020 also advocates for a more adaptable curriculum that permits students to explore various subjects across different fields, moving away from the traditional rigid academic tracks.

Moreover, the NEP emphasizes the importance of vocational training and prioritizes the development of critical thinking and problem-solving skills, aligning India's educational system with global standards while catering to the diverse cultural and socioeconomic fabric of the nation. The policy also underscores the value of multilingual education, promoting the use of native languages as mediums of instruction in early education. This approach not only respects India's linguistic diversity but also meshes traditional educational values with modern pedagogical strategies, enabling students from various backgrounds to learn effectively in their mother tongues while acquiring proficiency in additional languages, including English.

1.3 The Changing Role of Teachers in Modern Education

In the contemporary educational sphere of India, the transformation in the role of teachers is profound. Teachers are no longer seen merely as authoritative figures dispensing knowledge from textbooks; they have evolved into facilitators, mentors, and guides who support the development of critical thinking and problem-solving skills, which are crucial for navigating the complexities of the 21st century. This shift has been driven by an increasing awareness that education should extend beyond mere rote memorization and exam preparation. As the educational environment becomes more learner-centered, teachers are increasingly responsible for creating interactive learning spaces that foster curiosity, creativity, and collaboration.

Traditionally, the Indian educational system was characterized by a teacher-centric approach where the educator was viewed as the definitive source of knowledge, with students expected to passively receive, memorize, and regurgitate information. This model emphasized discipline and reverence for authority but often limited students' engagement with the material, suppressing their opportunity to question, explore, or develop analytical skills.

Today, however, the role of the teacher has been redefined to suit a more dynamic and interactive educational model. Teachers are now seen as facilitators of learning rather than mere transmitters of facts. They are tasked with encouraging students to take an active role in their own education, guiding them through processes of inquiry and collaborative learning. This paradigm shift is crucial in an era where information is ubiquitous and readily accessible via digital platforms. Teachers are no longer the sole custodians of knowledge; instead, they assist students in navigating vast information resources, helping them to discern, assimilate, and apply knowledge in practical and impactful ways (Figure 1.3).

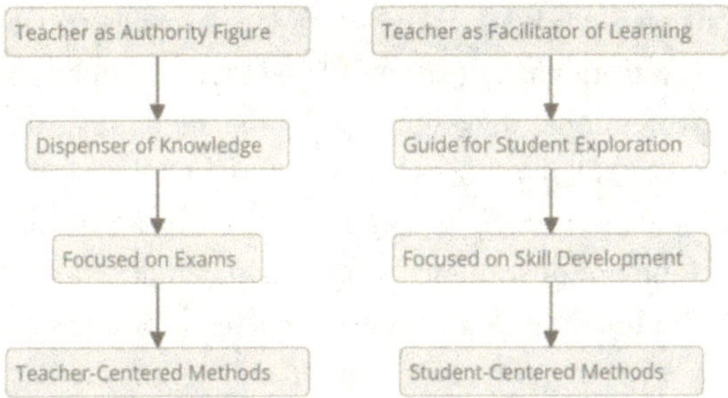

Figure 1.3: This diagram shows the evolving role of teachers in modern education:

- **Traditional Role**:
o **Teacher as Authority Figure**: The teacher was the central figure of authority in the classroom, focusing on being the primary dispenser of knowledge.
o **Exam-Focused**: Emphasis was on preparing students for exams through teacher-centered methods.
- **Modern Role**:
o **Teacher as Facilitator of Learning**: Teachers now act as guides in the learning journey, fostering an environment that encourages students to explore and discover independently.
o **Skill-Focused**: Focus has shifted to skill development and promoting critical thinking through student-centered methods.

The National Education Policy (NEP) 2020 has indeed catalyzed a significant transformation in the role of teachers within India's educational system. The policy underscores the importance of crafting holistic learning environments where teachers are central to nurturing not only academic prowess but also emotional and social development. The NEP 2020 champions experiential and inquiry-driven learning, encouraging teachers to design and implement lessons that ignite students' natural curiosity and actively engage them in addressing real-world issues. In this evolved role, teachers are expected to be versatile, adaptive, and innovative, utilizing a range of teaching methods to cater to the varied needs of their students.

Furthermore, the integration of technology in education has profoundly altered the traditional role of teachers. With the adoption of digital tools and online platforms, teachers are moving away from conventional lecture-based methods to embrace multimedia resources, interactive activities, and digital assessments that enrich the learning experience. This shift requires teachers to acquire and continually update their technological skills to stay effective in a rapidly changing educational landscape. The NEP 2020 emphasizes the necessity for continuous professional development for teachers, ensuring they are well-equipped to face the challenges of modern classrooms.

Beyond academic instruction, the evolving role of teachers involves fostering the holistic development of students, emphasizing emotional intelligence, social skills, and character building. Teachers are expected to create safe and supportive environments where students feel comfortable expressing their ideas and concerns. Acting as mentors, teachers guide students not only academically but also in their personal growth, helping them navigate peer relationships, self-esteem issues, and the pressures of contemporary life.

With a focus on inclusive education, teachers also play a critical role in ensuring equitable access to quality education for all students, including those with special needs. This requires teachers to be attentive to the diverse learning preferences and challenges of their students and to employ differentiated teaching strategies that accommodate individual capabilities. The NEP 2020 stresses the importance of inclusivity in education, advocating for teaching approaches that are accommodating, supportive, and welcoming to all learners, thereby promoting an educational environment that values diversity and fosters a sense of belonging among all students.

1.4 The Need for Innovation in Teaching for Indian Classrooms

In today's rapidly evolving educational landscape, particularly in India, the imperative for innovation in teaching has never been greater. Traditional educational methods, while providing a solid foundational base, fall short in preparing students for the multifaceted challenges of the modern world. Innovative teaching practices not only enhance the overall quality of education but also equip students with critical skills necessary for success in a dynamic, technologically driven, and globally interconnected economy.

The vast diversity within Indian classrooms, which include both urban and rural settings, necessitates creative and adaptable teaching strategies tailored to the specific needs of each student. A driving factor behind this push for innovative teaching is the increasing acknowledgment that education must transcend traditional rote learning and standardized tests. The National Education Policy (NEP) 2020 highlights the need to shift from a predominantly content-heavy curriculum towards one that fosters critical thinking, problem-solving, and creativity, promoting a more holistic development through experiential learning opportunities. For example, the policy encourages project-based learning, internships, and other practical experiences that allow students to apply theoretical knowledge in real-world scenarios. Such a paradigm shift compels educators to explore beyond conventional classroom boundaries and breathe life into their teaching methods.

Moreover, as students today have unprecedented access to digital information, it becomes essential for teaching methods to evolve to not only keep pace with technological advancements but also to help students critically engage with this information. The integration of technology in classrooms through smartboards, educational apps, and online platforms transforms traditional learning environments into interactive and engaging spaces. These tools provide personalized learning experiences that cater to individual learning styles, making education more inclusive and accessible.

The NEP 2020 acknowledges the potential of technology to democratize education by making high-quality educational resources available to students in even the most remote locations. It advocates for the utilization of e-learning platforms and digital tools to bridge the educational gap between urban and rural areas. This requires teachers to be proficient in integrating technology with their teaching practices, using multimedia to clarify complex concepts, employing data analytics to monitor student progress, and creating collaborative online environments for students to work together, irrespective of geographical boundaries.

Addressing the diverse learning needs of students is another crucial aspect of modern teaching. Today's classrooms are increasingly inclusive, accommodating students from various cultural, linguistic, and socio-economic backgrounds. Differentiated instruction allows educators to modify their teaching approaches to suit different learning preferences, ensuring that all students have equal opportunities to succeed. For instance, while some students may benefit from hands-on activities, others might find visual or auditory aids more effective.

Additionally, the approach to student assessment is undergoing significant changes. Traditional exams often focus narrowly on memorization and do not adequately reflect a student's comprehensive abilities. The NEP 2020 promotes competency-based assessments that evaluate students on their understanding and practical application of knowledge, not merely their memory. Innovative assessment methods such as open-book exams, presentations, group projects, and reflective writing offer students varied avenues to demonstrate their learning, emphasizing skills like critical thinking, teamwork, and problem-solving.

Furthermore, there is a growing emphasis on the importance of emotional and social learning. Innovative teaching practices that incorporate activities like mindfulness exercises, collaborative discussions, and social-emotional learning sessions are crucial in developing students' emotional intelligence, empathy, and interpersonal skills. These methods are particularly relevant in India, where academic pressures can be intense, and students benefit from tools that help them manage stress and build resilience.

1.5 Global vs. Indian Teaching Methodologies

Teaching methodologies around the world have undergone profound changes, with many countries adopting advanced, student-centered approaches that prioritize critical thinking, creativity, and collaboration. India is progressively aligning with these global trends, although the shift from traditional, teacher-led methods has been gradual and complex. While several international education systems have embraced flexible and experiential learning, significant segments of India's educational structure continue to focus on rote learning and examination-driven assessments. However, the introduction of the National Education Policy (NEP) 2020 ignites hope for a transformation in Indian classrooms that integrates global best practices while preserving unique cultural and educational traditions.

Globally, education systems in countries like Finland, Singapore, and the United States emphasize developing students' critical thinking, problem-solving abilities, and the practical application of knowledge. Here, the teacher's role has transitioned to that of a facilitator, guiding students through inquiry, discussion, and collaborative projects. Classrooms are interactive environments where students actively engage in their learning, often through group problem-solving and experimentation. Assessment methods in these systems focus on project-based evaluations, peer reviews, and continuous feedback, moving away from sole reliance on standardized exams.

Contrastingly, traditional Indian teaching methods have centered around teacher-led instruction, with the teacher positioned as the ultimate authority. Rooted deeply in the guru-shishya tradition, this method emphasizes discipline, respect for authority, and memorization. Although it has been effective in producing academically proficient students who excel in exams, it has faced criticism for limiting creative and critical thinking. Typically, student assessment focuses on the ability to memorize and reproduce information, with less attention on conceptual understanding and real-world application.

A notable difference between global and Indian teaching methods lies in technology integration. Internationally, education systems incorporate technology seamlessly into learning, using digital tools, online resources, and interactive platforms to enhance student engagement and offer personalized educational experiences. For instance, in countries like South Korea and Estonia, students regularly use digital platforms for accessing study materials, collaborating with peers, and receiving teacher feedback, allowing for a tailored educational path that accommodates individual interests and paces.

In contrast, while urban, particularly private, schools in India are slowly adopting technology in classrooms, most schools, especially in rural areas, continue to rely on traditional resources such as blackboards and textbooks. The digital divide remains a significant barrier, with many schools lacking the infrastructure, resources, and teacher training necessary to implement effective technology-driven teaching methods. The NEP 2020 addresses this issue by advocating for enhanced use of technology in education, promoting the development of e-learning platforms, mobile apps, and digital classrooms, especially targeting rural and underserved communities to ensure equitable access to quality education.

Furthermore, global education systems place a strong emphasis on student well-being and social-emotional learning. Countries like Canada and Finland recognize that education extends beyond academic achievement to encompass holistic student well-being. Their curricula integrate social-emotional learning, mindfulness practices, and mental health support, helping students develop resilience, empathy, and emotional intelligence.

In India, traditionally, less focus has been placed on these aspects of education. However, the NEP 2020 brings these elements to the forefront, advocating for a more comprehensive approach to learning that includes emotional and psychological development alongside academic instruction.

As India adopts these global teaching methodologies, it is imperative to balance them with the nation's unique cultural and educational contexts. The NEP 2020 seeks to blend modern educational practices with India's traditional strengths, such as incorporating diverse cultural heritage, languages, and indigenous knowledge systems into the curriculum. This integration ensures that students not only become globally competitive but also remain deeply rooted in their cultural identities, fostering the development of well-rounded individuals equipped for both local and global arenas.

1.6 Challenges of Implementing Novel Methods in India

The implementation of innovative teaching methods marks a crucial step in transforming India's educational system, although it introduces complexities, especially in transitioning from traditional methods to more student-centered approaches. The diverse educational landscape in India, characterized by disparities in resources, infrastructure, and teacher training between urban and rural areas, poses significant challenges in uniformly applying these innovative methods across all regions. Despite the ambitious visions of the National Education Policy (NEP) 2020, the true measure of success will be in its effective execution and the realization of quality education for every student.

One major challenge is the infrastructural divide between urban and rural schools. Many rural schools lack basic amenities like adequate classrooms, electricity, and internet access, hindering the adoption of technology-driven teaching methods. While urban schools, particularly private ones, may quickly embrace smart classrooms and digital tools, rural schools often struggle with outdated resources and limited access to technology. The NEP 2020 acknowledges these issues and proposes initiatives to enhance infrastructure in remote areas; however, substantial time and investment are required to effect significant change.

Another critical area is teacher training. The efficacy of innovative teaching strategies heavily relies on the capability of teachers to implement them effectively. In India, a significant number of teachers, particularly in government schools, are accustomed to conventional instructional methods focused on lectures and passive learning. Transitioning to interactive, student-centered methods necessitates that teachers acquire new skills, such as facilitating discussions, integrating technology into lessons, and fostering dynamic learning environments. The NEP 2020 underscores the need for ongoing professional development programs to equip teachers with these modern pedagogical skills.

Furthermore, the prevalent examination system, which primarily values rote learning and standardized testing, poses another hurdle. This system pressures students to achieve high scores rather than fostering a deep understanding and application of knowledge. The NEP 2020 advocates shifting towards competency-based assessments that evaluate students on their practical application of knowledge rather than mere fact recall. However, altering the entrenched perceptions of educators and parents, who often view exam success as the pinnacle of educational achievement, requires time and a cultural shift towards valuing creativity, problem-solving, and critical thinking over traditional metrics.

The digital divide also significantly impedes the implementation of technology-enhanced learning. Many students, especially in rural areas, do not have access to necessary digital devices or reliable internet connections. The NEP 2020 addresses this issue by suggesting solutions such as offline learning platforms and technological support for disadvantaged students, but bridging this gap will necessitate strategic, long-term planning and considerable investment to ensure equitable access for all students.

Additionally, the cultural and linguistic diversity of India complicates the adoption of uniform teaching methods. With a multitude of languages, cultures, and traditions, methods that are effective in one region may not be suitable in another. The NEP 2020 promotes the use of mother tongues or regional languages as mediums of instruction in early education to enhance inclusivity. This approach, however, demands that educators be proficient in multiple languages and adaptable to various cultural contexts.

Despite these obstacles, the introduction of innovative teaching methods presents an exciting opportunity for the evolution of Indian education. The NEP 2020 lays the groundwork for a significant transformation towards a more flexible, student-centered, and holistic approach. Emphasizing experiential learning, critical thinking, and creativity, the policy aims to prepare students with the skills necessary for success in a modern global environment. With sustained investment in infrastructure, teacher training, and digital accessibility, India has the potential to surmount these challenges and establish an education system that is both innovative and inclusive.

1.7 Government Initiatives and Educational Reforms in India

India's educational system has experienced significant evolution, driven by various governmental initiatives aimed at enhancing accessibility, quality, and inclusiveness. Recognizing the necessity for educational reform to meet global standards while catering to the diverse needs of its vast population, the Indian government has focused on creating a more equitable, learner-centric system. These reforms are designed to promote holistic development and equip students with the skills required for the 21st century. Guided by pivotal policies such as the Right to Education (RTE) Act and the more recent National Education Policy (NEP) 2020, these efforts have laid the groundwork for a forward-thinking educational landscape.

The RTE Act, implemented in 2009, marked a transformative moment by establishing education as a fundamental right for children aged 6 to 14, ensuring free and compulsory education. This act was pivotal in expanding access to education, especially for economically disadvantaged children, integrating millions of previously out-of-school children into the formal education system.

By emphasizing inclusivity, it laid the foundation for a more equitable and just educational framework. Additionally, the Sarva Shiksha Abhiyan (SSA) program, initiated in 2001, significantly contributed to promoting universal elementary education, focusing on ensuring access to education for every child, enhancing infrastructure, and facilitating teacher recruitment and training. This initiative notably boosted school enrollment rates and improved education quality, particularly in rural areas, setting the stage for further educational reforms at secondary and higher levels.

In recent years, the NEP 2020 has stood out as the most comprehensive reform in Indian education. It provides a detailed blueprint for revamping the education system to make it more flexible, multidisciplinary, and aligned with the demands of the 21st-century global economy. A key objective of the NEP is to shift away from rote learning, instead emphasizing critical thinking, creativity, and problem-solving. The policy champions experiential and skill-based learning, encouraging students to apply their knowledge in practical, real-world situations beyond mere fact memorization.

A significant emphasis of the NEP 2020 is on early childhood education, acknowledging that foundational learning is crucial for sustained academic success. It proposes a new educational structure (5+3+3+4), replacing the traditional 10+2 system, which starts with five years of foundational education focused on play-based and activity-based learning to enhance cognitive, emotional, and physical development from an early age. This shift aims to tackle learning gaps early on, ensuring a robust educational foundation for all children.

Moreover, the integration of technology into education is a central reform of the NEP 2020, recognizing the role of digital learning in democratizing access to quality education, particularly for remote and underserved areas. Initiatives like DIKSHA and SWAYAM provide free digital resources, helping students learn at their pace and offering teachers professional development opportunities. The government also promotes e-learning and hybrid models, blending online and traditional instruction to offer a more personalized educational experience.

Vocational education also receives significant attention in the NEP, with an aim to embed skills training within the core curriculum. This approach ensures that students acquire practical skills applicable directly to the workforce, bridging the gap between academic study and employability. Such initiatives are part of a broader governmental effort to cultivate a skilled workforce that can contribute effectively to India's economic advancement.

Teacher training and professional development are integral to the success of these educational reforms. The government has launched various initiatives, such as NISHTHA, to equip educators with modern teaching methodologies, enhance student-centered approaches, and facilitate the integration of technology into teaching, ensuring that teachers are well-prepared to implement these transformative educational strategies effectively.

1.8 Overview of Novel Teaching Approaches for Indian Classrooms

Innovative teaching methodologies are significantly reshaping India's educational landscape by transitioning from traditional, teacher-centered techniques to more student-focused, experiential models. These modern approaches aim to create engaging, interactive, and relevant learning environments that are better suited to the demands of the contemporary world. By emphasizing critical thinking, creativity, collaboration, and problem-solving, such methods prepare students to excel in a rapidly changing global environment. With the advent of the National Education Policy (NEP) 2020, these innovative techniques are becoming more prominent, marking a significant shift in both the delivery and perception of education throughout the nation.

A key strategy in this transformation is the flipped classroom model, which has begun to take hold in Indian education. This approach involves students first encountering new concepts through pre-class assignments like videos or readings, allowing them to engage with new material at their own pace. Classroom time is then devoted to deeper engagement through discussions, problem-solving, and group activities, fostering a more active and participatory learning environment. This model not only promotes a deeper understanding but also enhances student autonomy in their educational journey.

Project-Based Learning (PBL) is another method gaining ground in Indian schools. PBL immerses students in complex, real-world challenges, requiring them to draw on and integrate knowledge across various disciplines. Through this hands-on approach, students enhance their inquiry, research, and teamwork skills, acquiring vital competencies such as communication and collaboration. By linking theoretical knowledge with practical applications, PBL helps students see the relevance of their classroom lessons to real-life situations.

Additionally, collaborative learning techniques such as peer teaching and group projects are becoming increasingly prevalent. These methods encourage students to collaborate, share knowledge, and support each other's learning processes. Peer teaching, where students explain concepts to their peers, not only reinforces their own understanding but also improves their communication skills.

CHAPTER 2

ACTIVE LEARNING STRATEGIES

2.1 What is Active Learning in the Indian Context?

Active learning represents a significant paradigm shift in educational methodologies, moving away from the traditional model of passive absorption of information to a more dynamic, student-centered approach. In the Indian educational context, this transition marks a notable departure from the usual classroom dynamics where the teacher predominantly dictates the learning process, and students passively receive information through listening and note-taking. Active learning involves engaging students in discussions, problem-solving tasks, group collaborations, and practical exercises, which not only enhances their understanding of subjects but also bolsters critical thinking skills.

In Indian education, the adoption of active learning is particularly crucial as it aligns with the objectives set forth in the National Education Policy (NEP) 2020. This policy aims to shift away from rote learning to teaching strategies that enable students to apply knowledge in practical, real-world contexts. Active learning is instrumental in this educational transformation, facilitating independent thinking, collaborative work among peers, and creative problem-solving approaches.

The impetus for integrating active learning into Indian classrooms stems from evolving global workforce demands where skills such as critical thinking, problem-solving, and effective communication are increasingly valued. Traditional educational practices in India typically focus on evaluating students through their ability to memorize and regurgitate information during exams. While this method builds a solid knowledge base, it often falls short in developing the adaptability and innovative thinking needed for modern career paths. Active learning, however, prioritizes the cultivation of these vital skills, preparing students for the complexities of contemporary career landscapes and life challenges.

Active learning can take various forms in Indian classrooms. One common approach is through group discussions and debates, which encourage students to express their opinions, defend their ideas, and consider alternative viewpoints. This not only deepens their understanding of the subject matter but also improves their communication skills and ability to work collaboratively. Problem-based learning is another effective method, where students tackle real-life problems, promoting analytical thinking and linking theoretical knowledge with practical application (Figure 2.1).

The benefits of active learning extend across diverse educational settings in India, from urban to rural. In urban schools, where access to technological resources and modern instructional tools is generally better, active learning can be effectively combined with digital platforms, facilitating virtual collaborations and exploration of interactive multimedia resources. Meanwhile, in rural areas, despite often facing resource limitations, schools can still implement active learning through peer teaching, community-based projects, and experiential learning activities that make use of local resources. These approaches help to democratize education, ensuring that students from various backgrounds can benefit from enhanced learning experiences that are both engaging and relevant.

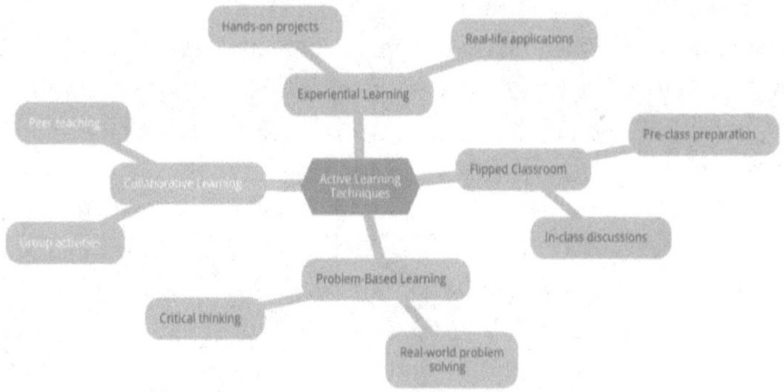

Figure 2.1: This mind map illustrates the key **Active Learning Techniques**:
- **Flipped Classroom**:
  o Pre-class preparation.
  o In-class discussions.
- **Problem-Based Learning**:
  o Real-world problem-solving.
  o Emphasis on critical thinking.
- **Collaborative Learning**:
  o Group activities.
  o Peer teaching.
- **Experiential Learning**:
  o Hands-on projects.
  o Real-life applications.

A significant challenge in implementing active learning in India is managing the large class sizes, particularly in government schools. Active learning thrives on a personalized approach, enabling teachers to provide individual attention and foster meaningful interactions. However, with classrooms often accommodating more than 50 students, achieving this becomes challenging. To address this, educators can utilize strategies like peer learning, where students collaborate in smaller groups to engage with the material. This approach helps make active learning more practical and effective, even in larger classroom settings.

Furthermore, the NEP 2020's emphasis on multilingualism during early education aligns well with the principles of active learning. Allowing students to study in their mother tongue or regional language enhances inclusivity and accessibility. This ensures that students can connect more profoundly with the material, as they are learning in a language they find familiar and comfortable.

2.2 Flipped Classroom Model: Indian Case Studies

The flipped classroom model presents an innovative approach to education by reversing the traditional sequence of instruction. In the conventional setup, teachers introduce new topics during class, while students reinforce their understanding through homework (**Figure 2.2**).

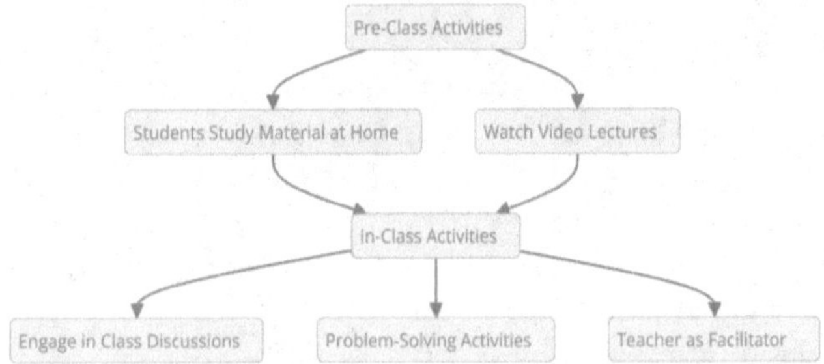

Figure 2.2: This flowchart illustrates the **Flipped Classroom Model** for Indian schools:

In a flipped classroom, the traditional process is inverted: students explore new concepts outside the classroom, often through pre-recorded lectures, assigned readings, or online materials. Class time is then dedicated to active engagement with the content through discussions, collaborative projects, and problem-solving activities. This approach has gained widespread recognition globally and is increasingly being embraced in India. It aligns effectively with the objectives of the National Education Policy (NEP) 2020, which advocates for experiential and skill-oriented learning.

Pre-Class Activities:

o Students study materials and watch video lectures at home.

- **In-Class Activities**:
  - o Focus on engaging in class discussions and solving problems with the teacher's support as a facilitator.

In India, the flipped classroom model has been effectively implemented across various educational settings, demonstrating its adaptability and effectiveness in enhancing student learning and engagement. This model reverses the traditional learning environment by delivering instructional content outside of the classroom and moving activities, including those that may have traditionally been considered homework, into the classroom.

In urban elite schools, particularly in cities like Bengaluru and Mumbai, this model thrives due to the availability of necessary infrastructure and technological resources. Private schools in these areas leverage the flipped classroom approach by integrating technology into learning, where students prepare at home through digital platforms like video lectures and interactive content. This preparation allows classroom time to be utilized for applying knowledge through advanced problem-solving, engaging discussions, and peer teaching. Such practices enhance critical thinking and problem-solving skills, essential for both academic and real-world success.

The Kendriya Vidyalayas (KVs), a network of government-operated schools across India, serve as another significant example. These schools cater primarily to children of central government employees and have piloted the flipped classroom model to elevate student engagement and understanding. Teachers in these schools provide students with video lectures and readings to be studied at home, which shifts the classroom focus to more interactive and participatory learning experiences. Early results from these pilot programs suggest improvements in student comprehension and increased participation in classroom activities, alongside more effective identification and remediation of learning gaps by teachers.

In rural areas, the application of the flipped classroom model faces challenges due to limited technological resources and inconsistent internet access. However, innovative adaptations have enabled its success. Teachers in these regions often employ a hybrid approach, using both offline resources like pre-recorded lessons and community-based educational strategies. In the classroom, the focus shifts to hands-on activities, discussions, and projects that link learning with community engagement, ensuring that students can practically apply their pre-learned knowledge.

The model has shown particular efficacy in STEM (science, technology, engineering, and mathematics) education, where understanding complex concepts is crucial. The ability for students to engage with theoretical material at their own pace at home, and then apply this knowledge in class through practical exercises, significantly enhances their grasp of difficult subjects. Reports from schools that have adopted this approach indicate notable improvements in STEM education, with students showing greater confidence and capability in managing complex problems.

The National Education Policy (NEP) 2020 supports the adoption of such innovative teaching methods, including the flipped classroom model. The policy emphasizes experiential and activity-based learning, which aligns well with the flipped classroom's focus on engaging students actively in applying their knowledge practically. Additionally, NEP 2020 advocates for enhanced integration of technology in education, recognizing that digital tools and e-learning platforms are crucial for the flipped classroom, allowing students to access instructional content from home and engage more profoundly during classroom sessions.

Despite its successes, the flipped classroom model faces significant challenges in India, especially in ensuring equitable access to technology. In rural and economically disadvantaged regions, the lack of reliable internet connectivity and digital devices remains a barrier to the model's widespread adoption. To combat these challenges, NEP 2020 includes initiatives aimed at reducing the digital divide, such as promoting affordable technology solutions and improving digital infrastructure in underserved areas, ensuring that all students can benefit from the educational advancements the flipped classroom model offers.

2.3 Problem-Based Learning (PBL) and Its Impact in India

Problem-Based Learning (PBL) represents a significant shift in educational methodology, focusing on students actively engaging with real-world issues to acquire knowledge, rather than relying solely on traditional lectures and passive learning. In India, PBL is increasingly valued for its ability to foster creativity, enhance problem-solving capabilities, and apply theoretical knowledge practically. These goals align well with the National Education Policy (NEP) 2020, which prioritizes experiential and skill-based learning.

In the Indian educational landscape, PBL is particularly beneficial as it encourages students to connect classroom theories to tangible, real-world challenges. Traditional educational practices in India often emphasize rote memorization, which can restrict the practical application of knowledge. PBL counters this by presenting students with complex real-life problems, pushing them to develop solutions that require a thoughtful application of what they have learned. This approach is essential for cultivating critical 21st-century skills such as critical thinking, collaboration, communication, and adaptability.

PBL is versatile and can be applied across various subjects. In science and mathematics, for instance, students might tackle engineering challenges, conduct environmental studies, or analyze data to form conclusions. These activities encourage students to move beyond textbook information, applying scientific and mathematical principles in collaborative, practical contexts. In the humanities, such as social studies, PBL can involve exploring historical events, societal issues, or economic challenges, fostering a deeper understanding of complex topics through active investigation and problem-solving.

In higher education, particularly in engineering and medical colleges, PBL has been effectively integrated into the curriculum to enhance hands-on learning. Institutions like the Indian Institutes of Technology (IITs) and top medical schools have adopted PBL to prepare students with practical skills applicable to their future careers. For example, engineering students might work on creating solutions for real-world engineering issues, while medical students might develop case studies to tackle healthcare challenges, applying their theoretical knowledge in practical, collaborative settings.

In primary and secondary schools, PBL is gradually being introduced to modernize teaching approaches and make learning more engaging and relevant. Teachers often assign projects that address local or community issues, requiring students to apply knowledge from multiple disciplines. A project on waste management, for example, might incorporate science (understanding decomposition), social studies (analyzing community behavior), and mathematics (calculating waste metrics). This kind of engagement not only deepens students' understanding of subjects but also illustrates the direct relevance of their studies to real-life situations.

PBL also plays a critical role in fostering innovation and entrepreneurship within India. By challenging students to think creatively and develop practical solutions to problems, PBL builds the confidence necessary for tackling complex challenges, an essential skill for entrepreneurs. Some educational institutions have extended PBL to entrepreneurship programs, encouraging students to turn project solutions into viable business ideas. This integration supports creativity and contributes to India's burgeoning startup ecosystem, equipping students with the entrepreneurial skills needed to drive innovation across various industries.

The NEP 2020 strongly supports the inclusion of PBL in the curriculum, emphasizing the development of critical thinking, creativity, and practical skills. By encouraging educational institutions to adopt PBL, the policy aims to move away from traditional exam-centric education towards more meaningful and impactful learning experiences.

2.4 Peer Teaching and Collaborative Learning Techniques in Indian Schools

Peer teaching and collaborative learning are increasingly recognized as transformative educational strategies that significantly enhance student engagement, comprehension, and cooperation in Indian classrooms. These methods shift the focus from individual competition to collective collaboration, allowing students not only to learn from each other but also to develop important social and cognitive skills. As traditional teacher-centered approaches may not fully equip students for the complexities of the 21st century, peer teaching and collaborative learning are gaining traction, particularly under the initiatives of the National Education Policy (NEP) 2020, which advocates for more interactive and student-centered educational practices.

Peer teaching involves students in roles where they share knowledge by explaining concepts, guiding each other through activities, or collaboratively tackling problem-solving tasks. This approach is mutually beneficial; the peer teacher consolidates their own understanding by articulating and organizing their knowledge, while the learner often finds complex subjects more accessible when explained by a fellow student. In the context of large Indian classrooms, where individual attention from teachers can be limited, peer teaching is invaluable. By forming pairs or small groups, students can work together on difficult material, making learning a collective endeavor.

A significant benefit of peer teaching is its capacity to foster communication and leadership skills among students. When students teach their peers, they are required to clarify their ideas, articulate their knowledge clearly, and respond to questions, which deepens their mastery of the subject. For the learners, receiving instructions from peers can provide insights that are more relatable and easier to understand, effectively overcoming educational hurdles. This reciprocal engagement not only boosts the confidence of peer teachers, who feel a sense of accomplishment, but also enhances the learners' clarity on challenging topics.

Contrastingly, collaborative learning involves students working together in groups to solve problems, complete projects, or engage in discussions. This setting encourages active participation in the learning process through the exchange of ideas, challenging of viewpoints, and exploration of concepts in depth. Collaborative learning is especially effective in promoting critical thinking, creativity, and teamwork-skills that are crucial for success in the contemporary world. In India's diverse and populous classrooms, collaborative learning enables students of varying backgrounds and skill levels to contribute to and benefit from the group dynamic.

A practical implementation of collaborative learning in Indian education can be seen in cooperative group projects. For example, in subjects like social science or environmental studies, students might investigate a local issue, gather data, and present their findings as a group. This process not only requires teamwork and delegation but also integrates research skills, enhancing their collective ability to work cohesively. In STEM fields, collaborative tasks such as complex problem solving or laboratory experiments allow each group member to bring their unique strengths and insights, enriching the learning experience for all.

The NEP 2020 strongly supports the adoption of these collaborative approaches, emphasizing a shift away from rote memorization to active engagement and problem-solving. The policy aims to foster critical thinking and communication skills among students, preparing them to tackle real-world challenges effectively. Moreover, it promotes inclusive educational environments where students from diverse backgrounds are encouraged to interact and learn collaboratively, enhancing social cohesion and mutual respect.

Technology plays a crucial role in facilitating peer teaching and collaborative learning. Digital tools and platforms enable students to undertake group assignments, share resources, and communicate beyond the classroom, which is particularly useful in rural areas where resources are limited. Platforms like DIKSHA and SWAYAM, endorsed by NEP 2020, facilitate peer-to-peer learning and virtual study groups, showing how technology can overcome geographical and resource-related barriers in education, making collaborative learning viable in a variety of educational settings.

2.5 Implementing Active Learning in Various Subjects in Indian Classrooms

Active learning methodologies can significantly enhance the engagement and understanding of various subjects in Indian classrooms, ranging from science and mathematics to languages and social studies. This approach, which shifts away from traditional passive listening and rote memorization to emphasize engagement, critical thinking, and hands-on experiences, is strongly aligned with the National Education Policy (NEP) 2020's focus on experiential and skill-based learning.

In the realm of science education, active learning transforms classrooms into vibrant learning environments where students explore scientific concepts through experiments, observation, and analysis. Practical activities, whether conducted in laboratories or as in-class hands-on projects, enable students to directly apply scientific principles in real-world contexts. For instance, a lesson on electricity could involve students in building simple circuits to understand how electrical currents work, moving beyond textbook explanations to actual experimentation. This method not only piques students' curiosity but also encourages a deeper engagement with the scientific process, perfectly complementing the NEP 2020's advocacy for inquiry-based science education.

Mathematics education benefits immensely from active learning, particularly through the use of Problem-Based Learning (PBL). PBL introduces students to real-life scenarios that necessitate the application of mathematical concepts and problem-solving skills. An example could be calculating the operational costs and potential profits of a hypothetical business, applying mathematical operations such as percentages, ratios, and algebraic functions. Collaborative problem-solving sessions, where students work together to approach complex mathematical problems, not only enhance their understanding but also show the practical relevance of mathematics in everyday life.

Language learning is another area where active learning strategies can have a transformative impact. Rather than relying on traditional methods like repetitive grammar drills or rote vocabulary memorization, language classrooms can benefit from integrating role-playing, group discussions, and creative writing exercises. These interactive activities encourage students to use language authentically and contextually, facilitating more effective communication and language acquisition. Peer teaching techniques, where students explain linguistic concepts to each other, also reinforce learning by requiring them to articulate their understanding clearly. The NEP 2020 supports such dynamic approaches to language education, particularly with its emphasis on multilingualism and practical language usage, making the learning process both more engaging and applicable for students.

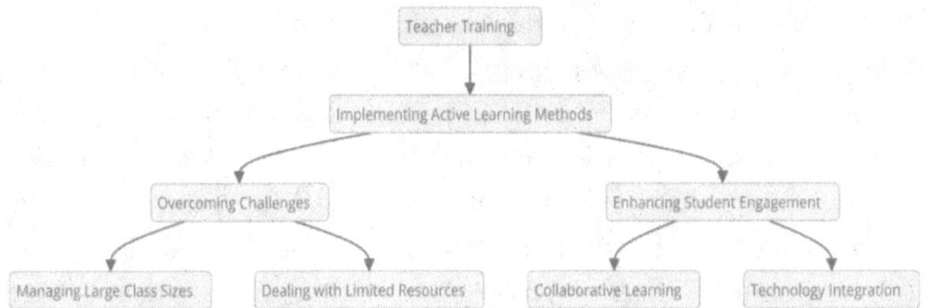

Figure 2.3: This flowchart outlines the key steps for **Implementing Active Learning in Indian Schools**:

- **Teacher Training**: Essential for preparing educators to use active learning techniques.
- **Implementing Active Learning Methods**: The core stage where active learning is integrated into the curriculum.
- **Overcoming Challenges**: Addressing issues like large class sizes and limited resources.
- **Student Engagement**: Enhancing engagement through collaborative learning and technology integration.

Active learning stands as a transformative approach within social studies, shifting away from the traditional memorization of dates, events, and facts towards a more engaging, project-based methodology that connects historical or social themes to contemporary issues. In this context, students examining the Indian independence movement might engage in a collaborative project that examines parallels between historical and modern social movements, thereby forging significant links between historical events and current societal challenges. Enriching the educational experience are activities such as debates, role-play simulations of historical scenarios, and projects rooted in community interaction. These techniques not only enhance the relevance of social studies to real-world scenarios but also deepen students' understanding of societal structures and historical dynamics, thereby preparing them to be well-informed, active participants in society.

Further application of active learning is evident in subjects like art, music, and physical education, where creativity, expression, and physical engagement are crucial. In art, for instance, students might delve into various techniques and mediums through direct, hands-on projects that explore aspects such as color, texture, and form. In music, active learning could encompass collaborative efforts to compose and perform pieces, while physical education might leverage team-based activities that enhance cooperation and strategic thinking. These areas, often perceived as secondary or supplementary, are essential to a comprehensive education, aiding in the development of a diverse skill set.

The National Education Policy (NEP) 2020 lays down a comprehensive blueprint for embedding active learning across various disciplines, advocating for an interdisciplinary and experiential educational approach. This policy champions adaptable curricula that fuse different fields of study and stress practical involvement, thereby ensuring a vibrant and pertinent learning experience. Teachers play a critical role in this educational evolution, tasked with creating and leading active learning endeavors that cater to varied learning preferences and promote student engagement. The NEP 2020 underscores the importance of ongoing teacher training to equip educators with the skills and resources necessary for the effective deployment of these educational strategies.

2.6 Overcoming Barriers to Active Learning in Indian Schools

The integration of active learning methodologies in Indian educational institutions is poised to significantly enhance the educational landscape by fostering a more interactive, engaging, and contextually relevant learning environment. Nevertheless, there are several impediments that need to be navigated to deploy active learning effectively. These include infrastructural deficits, the prevalence of large class sizes, conventional educational attitudes, and a lack of adequate teacher training. Despite these challenges, through strategic reforms proposed in the National Education Policy (NEP) 2020, Indian schools are well-positioned to surmount these barriers and fully leverage the benefits of active learning.

A primary obstacle is the issue of large class sizes, especially prevalent in public schools where class numbers often surpass 50 students. Active learning thrives on personalized engagement and small-group dynamics, which are inherently challenging in densely populated classrooms. To counteract this, schools might implement peer learning tactics, encouraging students to work together in small groups to delve into subjects and solve problems collaboratively. Moreover, adopting rotational models can allow different groups of students to partake in varied activities concurrently, thereby ensuring inclusive participation.

Another significant challenge is the deficiency in essential infrastructure and resources, particularly acute in rural areas. Many Indian schools are devoid of basic facilities such as adequate classrooms, consistent electricity, or technological access, all of which are crucial for active learning that often incorporates digital tools and hands-on activities. To mitigate these limitations, educators can employ locally sourced materials for experiential learning and utilize cost-effective or offline technological adaptations to facilitate interactive learning experiences. Additionally, government initiatives as per NEP 2020, like the enhancement of digital learning platforms including DIKSHA, are intended to bolster infrastructure and make educational resources more universally accessible.

The professional development of teachers also plays a pivotal role in the adoption of active learning. Many teachers in India remain anchored to traditional, lecture-centric teaching methods and may not be well-acquainted with active learning strategies. This paradigm shift necessitates teachers to transition to facilitators, orchestrating discussions, projects, and problem-solving activities rather than merely delivering content. Ongoing professional development is vital, and the NEP 2020 underscores the need for teachers to be equipped with contemporary pedagogical strategies, including active learning. Initiatives such as the National Initiative for School Heads' and Teachers' Holistic Advancement (NISHTHA) aim to aid educators in integrating active learning methodologies into their teaching practices. Supportive measures like mentoring and collaborative opportunities further facilitate this transition.

Additionally, a traditional educational mindset that prioritizes memorization and examination outcomes over critical thinking and creativity represents a significant cultural hurdle. In various regions of India, education is often viewed more as a pathway to excel in examinations rather than as a means to develop practical skills and knowledge. Active learning, which promotes inquiry, exploration, and cooperative learning, might be seen as detracting from exam preparation. Addressing this requires a cultural reevaluation of the intrinsic value of education, highlighting the long-term advantages of active learning such as enhanced critical thinking, problem-solving capabilities, and communication skills, rather than focusing solely on immediate examination performance. The NEP 2020 advocates for this transformation by endorsing competency-based learning and assessments that evaluate students' practical application of knowledge rather than rote memorization.

Challenges also persist in the implementation of active learning in traditionally lecture-driven subjects such as history or mathematics. However, inventive lesson planning can render these subjects more interactive and engaging. For example, history classes could incorporate role-playing or debates, and mathematics instruction might include problem-solving exercises or practical applications of mathematical principles. Integrative, cross-disciplinary methods can further amplify the relevance and engagement of active learning.

Finally, the digital divide remains a formidable barrier to the widespread adoption of active learning in India. While digital resources and platforms offer enriching interactive and multimedia learning experiences, access to necessary technological tools is often lacking, especially in rural locales. The NEP 2020 addresses this challenge by calling for enhanced investment in educational technology and advancing digital literacy. Government efforts such as SWAYAM and DIKSHA are designed to provide accessible digital resources, with ongoing initiatives aimed at improving internet connectivity and availability of digital devices in underprivileged areas. Community-based collaborations also contribute by offering communal resources like learning centers that provide technological access and foster active learning opportunities outside traditional school settings.

2.7 Teacher Training for Active Learning Methods

The successful rollout of active learning in Indian schools crucially hinges on the ability of teachers to effectively facilitate this approach. Active learning transforms the traditional role of educators from being mere deliverers of content to facilitators of student-centered learning, necessitating the acquisition of new skills and adoption of innovative educational strategies. The National Education Policy (NEP) 2020 highlights the critical importance of comprehensive and ongoing professional development for teachers to equip them with modern pedagogical techniques essential for active learning.

Active learning mandates that teachers foster environments where students actively engage with the material, collaborate with peers, and apply their knowledge in practical, problem-solving scenarios. This represents a substantial shift from the traditional lecture-based model that emphasizes passive absorption of information. In an active learning framework, teachers are expected to promote critical thinking, manage collaborative group activities, and encourage students to assume responsibility for their own learning, presenting significant challenges without adequate training.

Training for active learning should prepare educators to create interactive and participatory classrooms, develop activities that encourage student involvement, and employ strategies like group discussions, collaborative projects, and hands-on experiments. For instance, science teachers could be trained to lead inquiry-based activities that prompt students to investigate and hypothesize, while social studies might incorporate project-based learning to engage students with real-world issues.

Moreover, traditional assessment methods, which focus on rote memorization, do not align with the objectives of active learning that prioritize critical thinking and problem-solving. Teachers need training in alternative assessment strategies like formative assessments that provide ongoing feedback, including peer reviews and reflective journals, to better gauge student understanding and progress.

India's educational diversity, marked by disparities in resources and infrastructure, particularly in rural areas, further complicates the adoption of active learning. Teachers must be equipped with strategies to adapt these methods to varying contexts, using local resources or minimal technology. The NEP 2020 supports these adaptations by advocating for the integration of technology in classrooms and emphasizing the role of teacher training programs in facilitating effective use of such resources even in resource-scarce environments.

Transforming teachers' mindsets from traditional methodologies to embrace active learning is essential. Professional development must counteract resistance by demonstrating active learning's benefits, such as enhanced student engagement and academic outcomes. Successful examples and mentorship from peers can help in realizing these advantages.

The NEP 2020 provides a robust framework for teacher training, emphasizing continuous professional development to keep educators updated with the latest teaching strategies. Initiatives like the National Initiative for School Heads' and Teachers' Holistic Advancement (NISHTHA) are pivotal in equipping teachers with the necessary skills for active learning, thereby aligning with the NEP's objectives to foster experiential and skill-based learning.

By fostering a collaborative learning environment among teachers through sharing best practices and experiences, NEP 2020 facilitates a dynamic exchange of ideas and resources, further enriching the professional development of educators and enhancing the implementation of active learning across diverse educational settings.

2.8 Examples of Active Learning from Indian Education Systems

Active learning is increasingly recognized within the Indian educational framework, with numerous schools embracing this method to foster student engagement, critical thinking, and problem-solving abilities. This shift highlights the versatility and effectiveness of active learning across different subjects and geographical contexts, in line with the National Education Policy (NEP) 2020's focus on experiential and skill-based learning as pivotal elements of contemporary education.

A prime example of this approach is the implementation of project-based learning (PBL) in the sciences within urban educational settings, notably in cities such as Delhi and Bengaluru. Students in these schools engage in projects that tackle real-world problems, perform experiments, and exhibit their results. Science fairs in these institutions serve as platforms for students to work collaboratively on environmental challenges like waste management and water conservation, applying theoretical knowledge practically while enhancing creativity, teamwork, and communication skills.

The Kendriya Vidyalayas (KVs), a network of government-run schools across India, offer another illustration with their adoption of inquiry-based learning across various disciplines. In a historical context, students at one KV were engaged in exploring the socio-economic and cultural impacts of ancient Indian empires. Rather than rote learning, students examined primary sources, engaged in debates, and employed role-playing and presentations to convey their insights, thus making the subject more interactive and enhancing their analytical capabilities.

In rural settings, active learning is tailored to connect educational content with local community issues. For example, students in a Rajasthani village undertook a project to improve local water supply management. This involved collaboration with local authorities to monitor water levels and usage, leading to the development of viable community-based solutions. These initiatives not only reinforce classroom learning but also empower students to tackle pertinent local challenges, reflecting NEP 2020's aim to integrate local knowledge and make education more relevant and transformative.

At the tertiary level, premier institutions like the Indian Institutes of Technology (IITs) and the All India Institute of Medical Sciences (AIIMS) have integrated Problem-Based Learning (PBL) into their curricula. Engineering students at the IITs address real-world challenges through interdisciplinary methods, crafting innovative solutions, while medical students at AIIMS engage with clinical case studies, enhancing their diagnostic and collaborative skills. These practices prepare students for professional settings by emphasizing practical application of their knowledge.

Furthermore, technology plays a crucial role in promoting active learning across India. Educational platforms such as DIKSHA and SWAYAM offer free access to a wealth of resources and interactive content, enabling the integration of active learning strategies in schools and colleges.

CHAPTER 3

TECHNOLOGY-ENHANCED LEARNING

3.1 The Role of Technology in Indian Education

Technology has emerged as a transformative force within the Indian education system, fundamentally altering both teaching methodologies and student learning experiences. It extends beyond mere digitization of textbooks or online lectures, heralding a shift towards an interactive, personalized, and adaptable learning environment. This evolution aligns with the goals of the National Education Policy (NEP) 2020, which envisions making education more accessible, equitable, and responsive to the needs of the 21st century.

In urban Indian schools, the availability of advanced tools like smartboards, computers, and tablets has redefined educational interactions. Teachers leverage multimedia presentations, interactive quizzes, and digital simulations to demystify complex subjects and enhance student engagement. This shift from traditional chalk-and-talk methods to technology-infused instruction is particularly advantageous in subjects such as science and mathematics, where visual aids and interactive models significantly improve understanding.

A critical advantage of technology in education is its capacity to provide personalized learning experiences. Through adaptive learning platforms, students can progress at their own pace, concentrating on areas that require more attention. This personalized approach ensures that despite large class sizes, individual learning needs are addressed. Digital tools also offer immediate feedback, aiding teachers in pinpointing student weaknesses and providing specific support. This capability for real-time monitoring and tailored assistance, which was challenging to implement in traditional settings, marks a significant leap forward in enhancing educational outcomes.

Technology also plays a crucial role in bridging the urban-rural educational divide in India. In rural areas, where quality educational resources have traditionally been scarce, technology opens new avenues for learning. E-learning platforms, digital classrooms, and mobile apps now bring high-quality educational content to the most remote regions. Government-led initiatives like the DIKSHA platform offer free access to digital resources, ensuring that students in less advantaged areas have similar educational opportunities as their urban counterparts. This push towards democratizing education aligns with the NEP 2020's emphasis on equity and inclusivity, facilitating broader access to learning opportunities (Figure 3.1).

The COVID-19 pandemic accelerated the integration of technology into the Indian educational landscape. As educational institutions swiftly moved to online formats, technology became the primary conduit for instruction, reaching millions of students. This transition revealed challenges such as the digital divide and the scarcity of devices and reliable internet access in rural locales. Nonetheless, it underscored technology's critical role in sustaining educational continuity during disruptions. Many institutions are now adopting hybrid learning models, which combine traditional classroom teaching with online elements, fostering a more resilient and flexible educational framework.

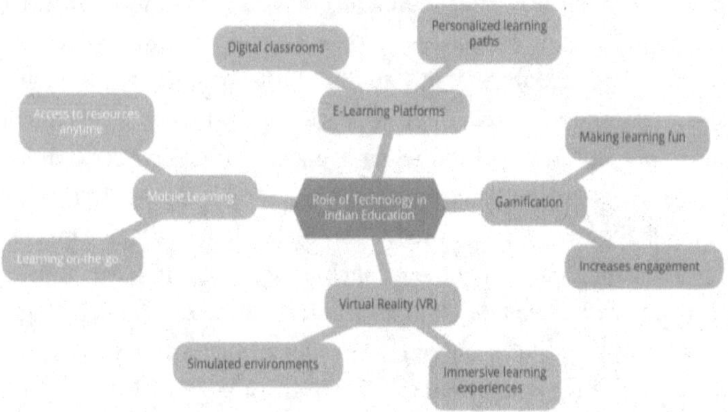

Figure 3.1: This mind map illustrates the **Role of Technology in Indian Education**:

- **Gamification:**
  - Using game mechanics to make learning fun.
  - Helps increase student engagement and participation.
- **Virtual Reality (VR):**
  - Provides immersive learning experiences.
  - Enables the use of simulated environments for teaching complex subjects.
- **Mobile Learning:**
  - Allows learning to on-the-go.
  - Students can access educational resources anytime, anywhere.
- **E-Learning Platforms:**
  - Creates digital classrooms for online learning.
  - Supports personalized learning paths to cater to individual student needs.

Additionally, technology has revolutionized the way teachers prepare and deliver their lessons. With a wealth of online resources at their disposal, including video tutorials, digital lesson plans, and collaborative tools, educators are empowered to significantly refine their instructional approaches. Platforms like SWAYAM and e-Pathshala, backed by the Indian government, offer free access to teacher training modules, facilitating the upskilling of educators and the adoption of contemporary teaching methods. The National Education Policy (NEP) 2020 emphasizes the critical role of continuous professional development for teachers, with technology acting as a pivotal medium to deliver such training extensively and efficiently.

Despite these advances, the integration of technology in Indian education faces notable challenges. The digital divide poses a significant hurdle, particularly in rural and economically disadvantaged regions, where many students lack access to digital devices and stable internet connections. While government initiatives are in place to mitigate these disparities, bridging this gap necessitates ongoing efforts and substantial investment. Moreover, it is essential to ensure that teachers are adequately equipped to utilize technological tools effectively. The varying levels of familiarity and comfort with digital resources among educators necessitate ongoing support and training to ensure that technology serves as an enhancer of educational quality rather than a source of new challenges.

3.2 Gamification in Indian Classrooms: Success Stories

Gamification in education is transforming Indian classrooms by integrating game-like elements such as rewards, points, challenges, and competition to make learning more engaging and enjoyable. This approach taps into students' inherent interest in games and competition, providing educators with innovative ways to render the learning process more dynamic, interactive, and student-centered. The National Education Policy (NEP) 2020 champions this method for its ability to enhance creativity, critical thinking, and problem-solving skills, making gamification a key strategy in modernizing education in India.

In urban schools, where digital tools are readily available, gamification is significantly altering educational experiences. Cities such as Bengaluru, Pune, and Delhi see schools embedding gaming elements into core subjects including mathematics, science, and languages. For instance, students might earn points for homework completion, problem-solving, or active participation in discussions. These points could lead to unlocking new challenges or earning digital badges, thus promoting a sense of achievement and enhancing motivation. This approach has proven particularly effective for engaging students who are typically less enthusiastic about conventional educational methods, offering them a rewarding and stimulating alternative.

A prominent example of successful gamification is the Byju's math education platform, which uses gamified modules to make math learning interactive and fun. Students accumulate points, badges, and position on leaderboards, making the subject more appealing and less daunting. Byju's has shown how gamification can transform challenging subjects into enjoyable ones, appealing to millions of students across India.

In rural areas, where resources may be scarcer, schools have implemented low-tech gamification strategies to captivate students. Educators employ physical activities such as quizzes, competitions, and role-playing to animate their lessons. For example, in subjects like social studies or history, teachers might conduct "historical trivia games" where students compete in teams to answer questions, enhancing teamwork, participation, and retention in an engaging, competitive format. These cost-effective methods underscore that gamification can be adapted effectively across various educational settings, even those with limited resources.

Further extending into life skills and social-emotional learning, some schools utilize gamification to teach empathy, teamwork, and conflict resolution. Role-playing games, where students assume different characters and navigate various social situations, foster emotional intelligence and communication skills, aligning with NEP 2020's objectives to diminish rote learning and promote comprehensive development through interactive learning experiences.

The language-learning app Duolingo exemplifies another success story in gamification, widely adopted by Indian students. Its game-like framework awards points, unlocks lessons, and encourages peer competition, enhancing language learning-a crucial component of NEP 2020, which emphasizes early multilingual education.

While the benefits of gamification are substantial, its integration into education requires meticulous planning and adequate teacher training. Some educators may perceive gamification as detracting from serious academic pursuits. To counteract this, professional development programs, as advocated by NEP 2020, should prepare teachers to effectively integrate gamification with traditional learning methodologies, ensuring that gaming elements complement rather than replace educational fundamentals.

Challenges related to access and equity also need addressing, particularly in under-resourced rural areas lacking necessary digital infrastructure. Creative, low-cost gamification approaches must be developed, and government initiatives aimed at enhancing digital accessibility are vital to ensure that the benefits of gamification reach all students, regardless of their socio-economic or geographical background, helping to bridge the educational divide across India.

3.3 Virtual and Augmented Reality for Education: Indian Context

Virtual Reality (VR) and Augmented Reality (AR) are rapidly emerging as transformative educational tools globally, and India is starting to tap into their potential. These technologies create immersive and interactive learning experiences that make complex subjects more engaging and accessible for students. Although VR and AR are still in the nascent stages of widespread adoption in India, they hold immense promise for enhancing educational practices, especially in areas where traditional methods fall short. With the National Education Policy (NEP) 2020 advocating for technology integration into education, VR and AR are poised to revolutionize learning across various subjects and educational levels in the country.

In traditional Indian classrooms, which often depend on textbooks and lectures, VR and AR introduce a compelling alternative by transforming abstract concepts into tangible experiences. For instance, VR can transport biology students on a virtual journey through the human bloodstream or allow them to examine body organs up close-experiences far beyond the scope of conventional diagrams. Similarly, AR can superimpose digital information onto physical objects in real-time, enabling students to interact with 3D models of molecules, historical structures, or geographic landscapes.

Several private schools in urban India, including those in cities like Bengaluru and Mumbai, are already integrating VR and AR into their curricula. These schools have set up VR labs where students can immerse themselves in virtual environments pertinent to their studies. For example, in history classes, students might undertake virtual tours of significant historical sites like the Taj Mahal or the ancient city of Harappa, thus gaining a more profound appreciation of India's cultural heritage through a vivid visualization of historical sites and events that textbooks alone cannot provide.

AR is similarly enhancing educational experiences in Indian classrooms. Science students, for example, can use AR apps to bring textbook diagrams to life in 3D, allowing them to manipulate models and view them from various angles to better understand complex scientific theories. AR also supports interactive quizzes and assignments, making the learning process more dynamic and engaging.

In rural India, where access to physical resources like laboratories and museums is limited, VR and AR can level the educational playing field. Students in remote areas can use VR headsets or AR-enabled mobile devices to access high-quality educational experiences similar to those available in urban centers. A rural school without a physical laboratory, for example, could use VR to conduct virtual scientific experiments, providing students with a hands-on learning experience that would otherwise be inaccessible. Likewise, AR can enable students to study historical artifacts or geographical features without the need to visit distant museums or sites.

The NEP 2020 emphasizes leveraging technology to enhance educational outcomes, and VR and AR fit perfectly within this framework. By facilitating experiential learning, these technologies help students deepen their understanding of subjects while promoting creativity, critical thinking, and problem-solving skills. Moreover, VR and AR can increase inclusivity in learning, offering alternative engagement methods for students with diverse needs, including those with visual or auditory impairments.

However, the adoption of VR and AR in Indian education faces challenges, notably the cost of technology. VR headsets and AR-enabled devices are currently expensive, placing them out of reach for many schools, particularly in economically disadvantaged areas. Nonetheless, as these technologies become more affordable and accessible, their adoption is expected to increase. Government initiatives aimed at enhancing digital infrastructure and equipping underfunded schools are crucial for broader implementation, as outlined in NEP 2020.

3.4 E-Learning Platforms and MOOCs in India

E-learning platforms and Massive Open Online Courses (MOOCs) have become essential in revolutionizing education in India by providing access to top-tier global learning resources. These platforms offer flexibility, affordability, and broad accessibility, addressing some of the inherent challenges of traditional classroom settings. As India continues to evolve its educational framework under the National Education Policy (NEP) 2020, e-learning platforms and MOOCs are instrumental in fostering inclusivity, increasing engagement, and meeting the needs of a digitally-driven era (Figure 3.2).

Among the standout examples of e-learning in India is SWAYAM (Study Webs of Active Learning for Young Aspiring Minds), a government-endorsed initiative. SWAYAM offers a wide array of free online courses covering numerous subjects, serving learners from school to advanced higher education levels. It is particularly aimed at bridging the educational gap between urban and rural areas, ensuring that high-quality educational materials are accessible to all, irrespective of geographical or socio-economic conditions. Featuring over 1,000 courses developed by esteemed institutions such as the Indian Institutes of Technology (IITs), Indian Institutes of Management (IIMs), and other leading universities, SWAYAM has established itself as a vital resource for students and educators alike, whether they seek to supplement classroom instruction or acquire new competencies.

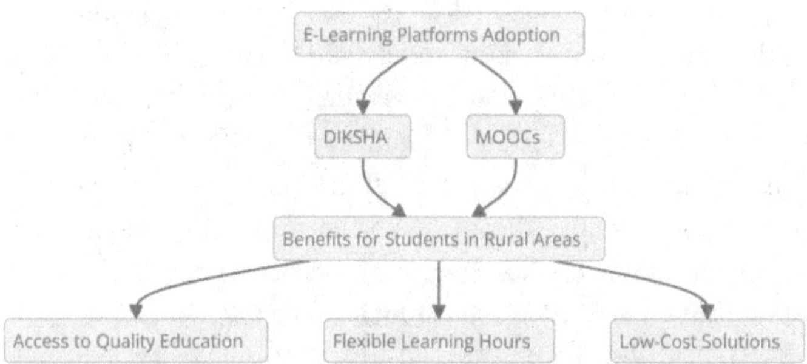

Figure 3.2: This diagram shows the adoption of **E-Learning Platforms** such as **DIKSHA** and **MOOCs** and their benefits for students, particularly in rural areas:

- **DIKSHA** and **MOOCs** are major platforms providing educational content.
- These platforms offer various **benefits for students in rural areas**:

o **Access to Quality Education**: Students can access materials that were previously unavailable.

o **Flexible Learning Hours**: Students can learn at their own pace and on their own schedule.

o **Low-Cost Solutions**: These platforms reduce the financial burden of education.

Massive Open Online Courses (MOOCs), provided through platforms such as Coursera, edX, and Udemy, have become increasingly popular in India. These platforms grant access to courses from prestigious universities around the world, enabling learners to study under experts across various fields. The expansion of MOOCs has democratized education within the country, affording students the opportunity to gain certifications and skills that were once out of reach due to geographic or economic barriers. For example, learners from smaller towns or rural areas can now access courses led by professors from top-tier institutions like Harvard, MIT, or Stanford, opening up previously unimaginable opportunities.

A key benefit of e-learning platforms and MOOCs is the flexibility they offer.

Learners can study at their own pace and choose their learning schedules, which is especially advantageous for working professionals or students with multiple commitments. This aspect of e-learning enables students to access quality education remotely, facilitating learning alongside other responsibilities. This advantage became even more pronounced during the COVID-19 pandemic when online learning emerged as the primary instructional method for many.

These platforms are also critical for teacher training and professional development. The National Education Policy (NEP) 2020 highlights the importance of ongoing professional development for educators. Platforms like SWAYAM and DIKSHA provide free resources that help teachers improve their instructional skills, adopt new pedagogical strategies, and keep abreast of current educational trends. These courses cover a wide range of topics, from classroom management to the integration of technology in teaching, helping educators navigate the evolving educational landscape.

Moreover, e-learning platforms and MOOCs enable personalized learning experiences. Leveraging data analytics and artificial intelligence, these platforms can track a learner's progress, pinpoint areas needing improvement, and suggest customized content to meet specific needs. This level of customization is difficult to achieve in traditional classroom settings, where a teacher must address the needs of many students simultaneously. E-learning allows for a focused and tailored educational experience, enhancing learning efficiency.

3.5 Mobile Learning and Internet Access Challenges in Rural India

Mobile learning, or m-learning, has become a pivotal aspect of education in India, fueled by the widespread adoption of smartphones and affordable internet. In rural areas, where traditional educational resources such as well-equipped schools and trained teachers are often scarce, mobile learning presents a transformative alternative. Utilizing mobile devices, students in even the most remote regions can access educational content, engage in online classes, and enhance their learning opportunities. This advancement is closely aligned with the National Education Policy (NEP) 2020, which prioritizes technology integration to make education more inclusive and accessible.

The suitability of mobile learning for rural India is particularly notable due to the extensive availability of smartphones, which are more accessible than other digital devices like computers or tablets. With the expansion of 4G networks and decreasing smartphone costs, students in under-resourced areas are increasingly able to use mobile devices to access educational materials. Educational platforms, apps, and online resources are readily available on smartphones, offering flexibility and adaptability to individual learning needs. This flexibility is crucial in rural settings, where students often balance educational activities with home or agricultural responsibilities, allowing them to learn at their own pace and convenience.

A significant benefit of mobile learning is its support for educational content in regional languages. Apps and platforms like Byju's and Khan Academy provide lessons in local languages, aligning with NEP 2020's focus on mother tongue instruction in early education, which helps students understand and retain concepts more effectively. Moreover, mobile learning applications frequently incorporate interactive elements such as videos, quizzes, and games, making the learning process engaging for students who may have limited formal education exposure.

Despite its advantages, internet accessibility remains a considerable challenge for mobile learning in rural India. Even as internet infrastructure expands, many remote areas still struggle with connectivity issues and low bandwidth, which can disrupt online learning. To counter this, several mobile learning apps offer offline functionalities that allow users to download content in advance and access it without needing an internet connection, ensuring continuous learning even in areas with unreliable internet services.

The cost of data plans also poses a barrier, particularly for low-income families in rural regions. Although smartphones have become more affordable, the expense of data for video-based learning can still be prohibitive. In response, the Indian government and telecom companies have launched initiatives to make data more affordable for educational use. Projects like BharatNet aim to deliver high-speed internet to rural villages, enhancing the feasibility of mobile learning in these communities.

Digital literacy is another critical factor for the success of mobile learning. While younger individuals may be more adept at using smartphones, not all students or their parents are familiar with navigating mobile learning platforms or apps. This lack of familiarity can hinder the effectiveness of mobile learning, making it challenging for users to fully engage with online resources or educational applications. To address this, digital literacy campaigns have been implemented to educate students and teachers on the effective use of mobile devices for educational purposes.

Mobile learning also plays a crucial role in the professional development of teachers in rural areas. Teachers in remote locations often lack access to ongoing training opportunities, but mobile platforms can connect them to a wealth of online courses, webinars, and workshops. By engaging in mobile learning, teachers can update their pedagogical skills and enhance their instructional capabilities, benefiting both themselves and their students. This dual applicability of mobile learning for both student education and teacher training underscores its potential as a transformative tool for bridging educational gaps in rural India.

3.6 Integrating Technology with Traditional Teaching in India

Integrating technology with traditional teaching methods in India signifies a significant shift towards creating more dynamic and engaging learning environments. This hybrid model combines the strengths of conventional education-such as direct interaction, classroom management, and personalized instruction-with the benefits of technological advancements, including interactive content, tailored learning paths, and immediate feedback. The National Education Policy (NEP) 2020 emphasizes the importance of merging technology with traditional pedagogy to enhance the accessibility, comprehensiveness, and efficacy of education.

Traditionally, Indian classrooms have depended heavily on teachers as the main conduits of knowledge, with students expected to passively absorb information. However, with the growing integration of technology, the role of teachers is evolving. They are transitioning from being the sole providers of knowledge to facilitators who support and guide students' learning journeys, encouraging exploration and active engagement with content. Digital tools like smartboards, multimedia presentations, and educational apps are instrumental in this shift, making lessons more vivid and enriching the educational experience.

One effective way to integrate technology into traditional teaching in India is through the use of digital learning platforms. Platforms such as DIKSHA and SWAYAM allow teachers to enhance their classroom teachings with supplemental videos, quizzes, and interactive activities that make complex subjects more comprehensible. For instance, a biology teacher might enhance a lesson on the human circulatory system with a video demonstration, offering students a visual representation of how blood circulates throughout the body. This approach supports various learning styles, ensuring that students who might find text-heavy materials challenging can still understand and retain complex concepts through visual and auditory means.

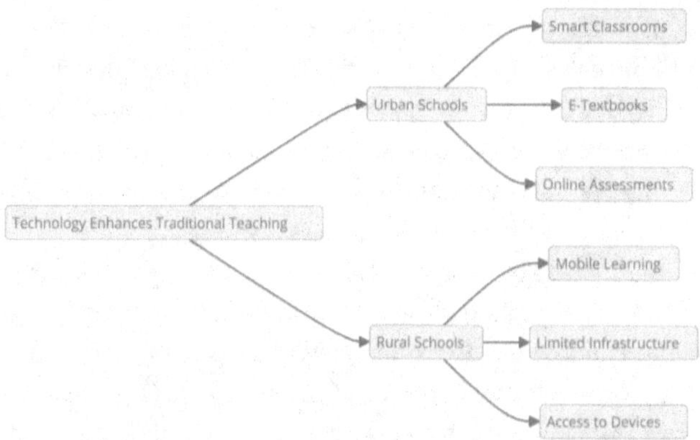

Figure 3.3: This flowchart shows how technology enhances traditional teaching in **Urban vs. Rural Schools**:

- **Urban Schools**:
  o Use of **Smart Classrooms, E-Textbooks**, and **Online Assessments**.
- **Rural Schools**:
  o Focus on **Mobile Learning** for access to educational content.
  o Face challenges such as **Limited Infrastructure** and **Access to Devices**.

Blended learning models are gaining traction in Indian schools, melding traditional lectures with online resources and assignments. This approach enables students to engage with learning materials at their own pace outside of class, providing flexibility to revisit challenging topics or explore subjects more deeply. In-class sessions are then dedicated to interactive activities like group discussions or problem-solving exercises, fostering a collaborative application of knowledge. This shift from teacher-led instruction to a student-centered model aligns with the National Education Policy (NEP) 2020, which promotes active and engaged learning environments.

Moreover, the integration of technology with traditional teaching is transforming assessment methods in Indian schools. Rather than solely relying on written exams, educators can utilize digital tools for real-time assessments. Online quizzes, interactive assignments, and data analytics enable continuous monitoring of student progress and immediate feedback. This approach allows for the early identification of learning gaps, facilitating timely interventions and personalized support. Additionally, digital tools can provide differentiated assignments, tailored to individual student needs, supporting personalized learning trajectories.

In rural India, where educational resources are often scarce, the fusion of technology with traditional teaching methods holds significant promise for reducing educational disparities (Figure 3.3). E-learning platforms and digital content can equip teachers in remote areas with high-quality instructional materials otherwise unavailable locally. For example, rural schools with limited lab facilities might employ virtual lab simulations to provide practical, hands-on science experiences that are typically inaccessible.

However, the successful implementation of technology in traditional teaching requires robust teacher training and infrastructure. Many educators, particularly in government schools, may lack familiarity with digital tools. To address this gap, NEP 2020 emphasizes the importance of continuous professional development. Training programs are being introduced to help teachers effectively integrate technology into their teaching, enhancing rather than replacing traditional methods.

Infrastructure challenges persist, particularly in rural areas, where schools might struggle with unreliable power supplies and limited access to digital devices. Government initiatives like BharatNet are crucial in expanding internet connectivity and reducing these disparities, ensuring that schools across India can benefit from technological advancements.

Subjects such as mathematics and science have shown particular success with this hybrid approach. Interactive simulations help students visualize complex mathematical functions or scientific processes, making abstract concepts more accessible. In language learning, digital tools like language apps and online dictionaries aid in vocabulary expansion and pronunciation practice, supplementing traditional grammar instruction. This blended methodology not only deepens student understanding but also increases engagement across various disciplines.

3.7 Government Policies and Support for EdTech in India

Government policies and initiatives have been pivotal in incorporating educational technology (EdTech) in India, significantly enhancing the accessibility, inclusiveness, and effectiveness of education. Recognizing EdTech's potential to address the disconnect between traditional education methods and contemporary learning demands, the Indian government has implemented various strategies in line with the National Education Policy (NEP) 2020. These measures are designed to foster a flexible, student-focused, and future-ready education system.

A key government initiative is the DIKSHA platform (Digital Infrastructure for Knowledge Sharing), introduced by the Ministry of Education. DIKSHA serves as a digital repository filled with learning resources like videos, worksheets, assessments, and textbooks, available to both students and teachers across the nation. This platform enriches traditional classroom settings with high-quality digital content available in multiple languages, proving especially beneficial in rural and underserved regions. It also supports teacher professional development, offering modules to help educators effectively incorporate technology into their teaching.

Another notable initiative is the SWAYAM platform (Study Webs of Active Learning for Young Aspiring Minds), which provides free online courses spanning from school education to higher education and vocational training. SWAYAM democratizes education by ensuring that quality learning opportunities are accessible to everyone, regardless of their geographical location or socio-economic status. The platform includes courses from prestigious institutions like the Indian Institutes of Technology (IITs) and Indian Institutes of Management (IIMs), facilitating access to top-tier education at no cost.

The NEP 2020 outlines a comprehensive approach for integrating EdTech into the Indian education framework, highlighting technology as a crucial facilitator of education. The policy encourages the widespread adoption of digital platforms, online resources, and educational apps to create more interactive and engaging learning environments. It also stresses the importance of digital literacy for both students and teachers, recognizing its significance for future learning and employment opportunities.

In support of these educational technologies, the government has launched initiatives like e-Pathshala, a digital library managed by the National Council of Educational Research and Training (NCERT) that offers textbooks and supplemental materials online. This initiative helps reduce dependency on physical textbooks and extends resource access, particularly in regions with limited educational materials.

The BharatNet initiative is vital for expanding broadband connectivity to rural areas, facilitating high-speed internet access for villages across India. This infrastructure development is crucial for enabling students in remote areas to utilize online learning platforms and access digital content and virtual classrooms, thereby bridging the digital divide.

Moreover, the government encourages private sector involvement in the EdTech space. Indian EdTech startups such as Byju's, Unacademy, and Vedantu have become significant contributors, offering innovative learning solutions that cater to the diverse needs of Indian students. Partnerships between these private entities and public initiatives promote innovation and scalability, helping to extend technology-driven learning solutions to a wider audience.

Teacher training and professional development remain central to the government's EdTech strategy. With NEP 2020 prioritizing continuous professional development, initiatives like NISHTHA (National Initiative for School Heads' and Teachers' Holistic Advancement) are crucial. They provide educators with the necessary tools and knowledge to effectively use digital resources, aiming to enhance the interactive and engaging nature of learning environments.

EdTech's influence extends into higher education as well, with the integration of virtual labs, online courses, and digital libraries into college and university curricula. Additionally, the government's focus on vocational education and skills training through digital platforms highlights EdTech's role in preparing students for the workforce, ensuring they possess the skills required to thrive in a rapidly changing job market.

3.8 Evaluating the Effectiveness of Technology-Enhanced Learning in Indian Schools

The integration of technology into Indian classrooms has markedly transformed the educational landscape, introducing innovative methods that enhance student engagement, personalize learning experiences, and expand access to resources. As technological adoption in education grows, it is vital to evaluate its effectiveness in improving student outcomes, refining teaching methodologies, and meeting the diverse needs of India's vast student body. The National Education Policy (NEP) 2020 endorses the use of technology to modernize education; however, assessing its impact requires both qualitative and quantitative indicators.

A fundamental metric for evaluating the effectiveness of technology-enhanced learning is its influence on student outcomes. In numerous Indian schools, the implementation of digital tools such as smartboards, educational apps, and online platforms has heightened student engagement. Interactive techniques, including quizzes, videos, and simulations, have proven successful in demystifying complex concepts. For instance, in subjects like science and mathematics, students often comprehend better when they can visualize processes through digital simulations or participate in interactive problem-solving. Teachers report increased participation and curiosity among students when employing these technological tools.

Personalized learning represents another critical domain where technology demonstrates significant potential. Adaptive learning technologies on digital platforms can tailor educational content to the individual pace and comprehension level of each student, addressing specific learning needs effectively. This is particularly beneficial in India, where classroom sizes can be large, allowing teachers to offer more focused support. Platforms such as Byju's and Khan Academy utilize data analytics to track student performance and provide personalized learning recommendations, leading to marked improvements in traditionally challenging subjects like mathematics and physics.

Moreover, technology has broadened educational access, especially in rural and underserved areas. Platforms such as DIKSHA and SWAYAM deliver high-quality educational materials nationwide, irrespective of geographic constraints. These platforms often provide content in multiple languages, supporting NEP 2020's focus on mother-tongue instruction, thus making education more inclusive. Additionally, the availability of offline learning options ensures continuous educational opportunities for students in regions with limited internet connectivity. This feature became particularly critical during the COVID-19 pandemic, when reliance on online learning intensified due to school closures.

CHAPTER 4

DIFFERENTIATED INSTRUCTION

4.1 Understanding Differentiated Instruction in India

Differentiated instruction is a teaching approach that recognizes and caters to the diverse learning needs of students within a classroom. In India, where classrooms frequently encompass students with varied abilities, learning styles, and cultural backgrounds, differentiated instruction is seen as a vital strategy for enhancing inclusivity and effectiveness in education. The National Education Policy (NEP) 2020 underscores the importance of flexible and personalized teaching methods, positioning differentiated instruction as a key component in India's vision for a more student-centered education system.

At its essence, differentiated instruction involves customizing lessons to meet the specific needs of each student by modifying the content, process, or outcome of learning. This method ensures that all students, regardless of their initial skill levels, can engage with and benefit from the educational material. In India's large and diverse classrooms, differentiated instruction enables teachers to create learning experiences tailored to different abilities, interests, and readiness levels, helping to ensure that no student is left behind and that every learner has the opportunity to succeed.

The significance of differentiated instruction in India is driven by an increasing acknowledgment of students' varied needs. Classrooms often contain students from disparate socio-economic backgrounds, linguistic groups, and learning abilities. While some students thrive in traditional lecture-based settings, others may need more interactive approaches, such as hands-on activities, visual aids, or additional support. Differentiated instruction allows teachers to address these varied needs by providing diverse learning options specifically designed for individual students.

In practical application, differentiated instruction in Indian classrooms might mean offering multiple ways for students to understand the same concept. For example, in a mathematics class, while some students might engage in independent problem-solving, others might benefit more from guided instruction or collaborative learning with peers. Teachers might employ a range of resources, including videos, worksheets, and interactive activities, to suit different learning preferences and styles. This flexibility not only boosts student engagement but also fosters a more inclusive learning atmosphere.

The NEP 2020 reinforces the importance of differentiated instruction by urging schools to move beyond traditional, one-size-fits-all teaching approaches. It advocates for personalized learning pathways that reflect the unique strengths and requirements of each student. This is particularly essential in Indian classrooms, where there is often a wide disparity in student preparedness and ability. Differentiated instruction addresses these differences by providing specific support to students who may struggle with particular concepts while allowing more advanced learners to delve deeper into subjects. This approach not only improves individual learning outcomes but also advances equity and inclusivity in education.

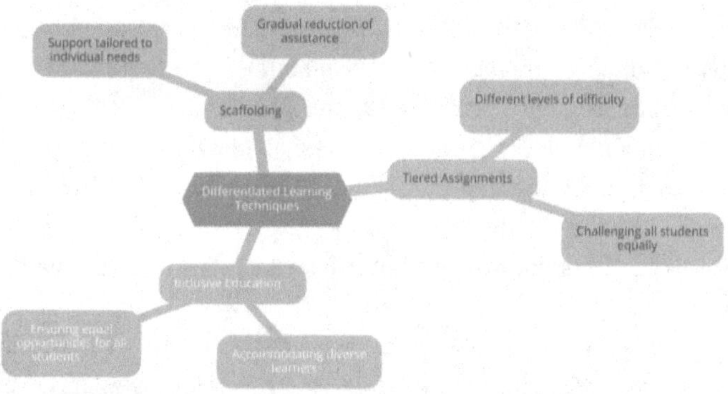

Figure 4.1: This mind map illustrates the various **Differentiated Learning Techniques**:

- **Scaffolding:**
  o Provides tailored support for students based on individual needs.
  o Gradually reduces assistance as students become more independent.
- **Tiered Assignments:**
  o Assigns tasks at different levels of difficulty to suit student abilities.
  o Ensures all students are challenged appropriately.
- **Inclusive Education:**
  o Accommodates learners from diverse backgrounds and abilities.
  o Ensures equal opportunities for all students.

Differentiated instruction seamlessly dovetails with the mandates of the National Education Policy (NEP) 2020, which stresses experiential and skill-based learning. This pedagogical strategy allows teachers to furnish students with varied interactive modalities for engaging with course content, thereby crafting learning experiences that are not only pertinent but also substantial. For example, in a social studies curriculum, students might be given the choice to articulate their understanding through diverse formats such as a research paper, a digital presentation, or a structured debate. This methodological flexibility not only plays to individual student strengths but also cultivates deeper cognitive engagement and bolsters critical analytical skills.

However, the practical implementation of differentiated instruction in Indian educational settings is fraught with challenges, particularly due to the prevalent issue of large class sizes. The typical classroom scenario often involves one teacher managing between 40 to 50 students, which can significantly hinder the personalization of instruction. Despite these obstacles, effective strategies and educational tools can facilitate the incorporation of differentiated instruction within these constraints. Group work, peer-assisted learning, and the strategic use of educational technology are instrumental in this regard. For instance, digital platforms can offer adaptive learning experiences through customized quizzes and modular lessons tailored to meet the individual comprehension levels of each student, thereby enhancing the educational efficacy for a diverse student body.

4.2 Tailoring Lessons to Individual Learning Styles in a Diverse Indian Classroom

Indian classrooms are notably diverse, hosting students with varied abilities, backgrounds, and learning preferences. This diversity necessitates adaptable teaching strategies to ensure all students have equal opportunities to succeed. Differentiated instruction, which tailors lessons to individual learning styles, is becoming increasingly valued in India as educators shift from traditional one-size-fits-all approaches. By customizing lessons for visual, auditory, and kinesthetic learners, teachers enhance engagement and effectiveness, creating a more inclusive learning environment.

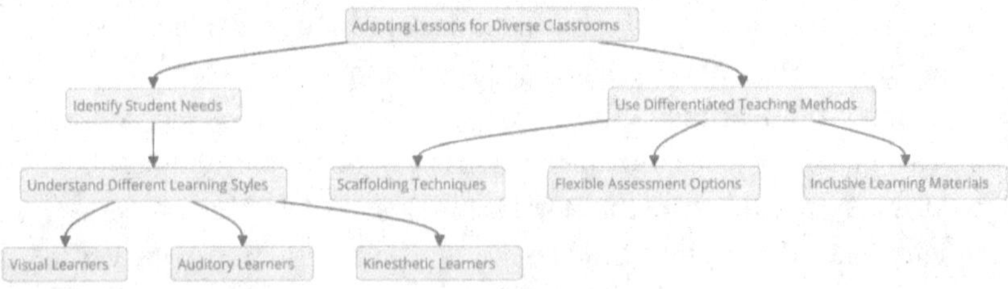

Figure 4.2: This flowchart shows how teachers can adapt lessons for **Diverse**

Classrooms in India:
- **Identify Student Needs**: Recognizing individual differences in learning preferences and needs.
- **Understand Learning Styles**: Catering to visual, auditory, and kinesthetic learners.
- **Use Differentiated Methods**: Applying scaffolding, flexible assessment, and inclusive learning materials to suit all students.

In India, classrooms feature a wide array of learning styles and academic readiness. Students may excel using visual aids like diagrams and videos, auditory methods such as discussions, or through kinesthetic activities like hands-on experiments. Adapting to these varied learning preferences is crucial for educational efficacy. For example, in teaching photosynthesis, a teacher might use animations for visual learners, discussions for auditory learners, and model-building for kinesthetic learners. This multifaceted approach ensures that all students, regardless of their preferred learning style, can access and engage with the material effectively (Figure 4.2).

The National Education Policy (NEP) 2020 advocates for such flexibility in teaching methods, promoting student-centered and adaptable learning experiences. It encourages educators to personalize lessons to accommodate the diverse educational needs characteristic of India's multifaceted student population. This is particularly pertinent given the wide range of linguistic and cultural backgrounds in Indian classrooms, where personalized lessons can help bridge the gap between students' home environments and their educational experiences.

Technology significantly aids in tailoring lessons to different learning styles. Digital tools and platforms provide varied resources, such as interactive simulations for kinesthetic learners and videos for visual learners. For auditory learners, podcasts and online forums can enhance understanding, supporting educators in creating inclusive and diverse instructional environments.

Peer learning and group activities also play a vital role by allowing students to learn from each other's strengths. In a diverse classroom, a student proficient in verbal explanation can assist a peer, while another who is visually oriented might use diagrams to clarify concepts. This collaborative method not only enhances learning but also fosters a community of mutual support, which is invaluable in India's large and heterogeneous classrooms.

4.3 Scaffolding and Tiered Assignments for Indian Students

Scaffolding and tiered assignments are crucial strategies in differentiated instruction, particularly relevant in Indian classrooms where students display diverse academic abilities, backgrounds, and learning styles. These methodologies ensure that all students, regardless of their skill level, can engage with educational content effectively and achieve academic growth. The National Education Policy (NEP) 2020 recognizes the importance of these strategies in creating a flexible, student-centered education system that accommodates the varied needs of learners.

Scaffolding in education involves breaking down learning into smaller, manageable segments, providing structured support that is gradually withdrawn as students gain independence. For instance, in a mathematics class on fractions, a teacher may initially guide students through basic concepts like numerators and denominators. As students become more competent, the teacher scales back assistance, encouraging learners to tackle more complex problems independently. This method not only helps students grasp difficult concepts but also fosters confidence and autonomy in learning. Additionally, scaffolding can incorporate various resources such as visual aids, hands-on activities, and collaborative tasks to accommodate different learning modalities.

Tiered assignments, another effective differentiation tool, involve creating variations of the same task to cater to different ability levels within the classroom. Each student works towards the same learning objective but at a level of complexity suited to their individual skills. For example, in an English class focusing on essay writing, more advanced students might write a complete essay, while others might work on structuring ideas or writing paragraphs. This approach ensures that tasks are appropriately challenging for each student, maintaining engagement and preventing frustration.

Such tiered assignments are especially beneficial in heterogeneous classrooms, common in India, where students may vary widely in their prior knowledge or language proficiency. These assignments keep students motivated by providing a sense of achievement as they complete challenges that are suitably demanding yet achievable.

Furthermore, tiered assignments promote inclusion by ensuring that all students, including those with learning disabilities or special needs, can participate effectively in learning activities. Tasks designed at varying levels of difficulty allow students to progress at their own pace while striving towards common educational goals, creating an inclusive environment where every student has the opportunity to succeed.

The integration of technology enhances the implementation of both scaffolding and tiered assignments. Digital tools and e-learning platforms enable personalized learning experiences that adjust to the readiness levels of individual students. Educational apps with adaptive features, for example, can modify the difficulty of quizzes based on student responses, allowing for customized progression. Digital resources also facilitate the creation of tailored assignments that cater to diverse student needs, ensuring that educational materials are accessible and appropriate for all learners.

4.4 Addressing Diverse Learning Needs Across Urban and Rural India

India's education system faces the significant challenge of catering to a diverse student population spread across urban and rural areas, each presenting distinct educational needs and conditions. This diversity necessitates a flexible and inclusive approach to teaching that can effectively adapt to the varied strengths and challenges of students from different backgrounds. Differentiated instruction emerges as a critical strategy in bridging the educational disparities between urban and rural settings, ensuring that all students, irrespective of their geographic or socio-economic status, access high-quality educational experiences.

In urban areas, students typically enjoy better access to resources like advanced technology, well-equipped classrooms, and a range of extracurricular activities. These advantages allow for a variety of teaching methods, such as technology-enhanced learning and project-based activities, which cater to diverse learning preferences and capabilities. However, urban classrooms still exhibit a range of academic abilities and socio-economic backgrounds, necessitating personalized learning approaches. For instance, differentiated instruction in these environments might involve providing complex problem-solving tasks to advanced students in mathematics, while offering scaffolded learning supports or peer tutoring to those requiring more foundational help.

Conversely, rural schools often grapple with challenges such as limited infrastructure, teacher shortages, and scarce digital tools, which can impede students' educational progress compared to their urban counterparts. Differentiated instruction in these settings focuses on maximizing the available resources to tailor support for students. Teachers might utilize local materials for teaching core subjects like science or math, turning everyday objects into educational tools, or employing strategies like scaffolding and tiered assignments to enhance student engagement and confidence.

The National Education Policy (NEP) 2020 prioritizes the reduction of educational disparities between urban and rural students and supports the adoption of differentiated teaching methods tailored to meet specific student needs. A key element of this strategy involves integrating technology to extend quality educational materials to rural areas. Platforms such as DIKSHA and SWAYAM, which offer a plethora of digital learning resources in multiple languages, are pivotal in this regard. This is particularly beneficial for rural students, enabling access to comprehensive educational content in their mother tongue, thus facilitating easier and more effective learning.

Addressing linguistic diversity is also crucial, especially in rural areas where many students speak regional languages at home. Differentiated instruction helps accommodate these students by adapting lessons to support multilingual learning environments, incorporating strategies like visual aids, simplified instructions, or bilingual resources. Early education in the mother tongue, as advocated by NEP 2020, helps students develop strong foundational language skills before transitioning to additional languages.

Furthermore, both urban and rural classrooms can benefit from group work and peer learning, which promote collaborative and supportive educational environments. In rural areas, where teacher resources may be stretched thin, peer learning is invaluable in ensuring that students support each other's educational journeys. In urban settings, where access to digital tools is more prevalent, technology facilitates personalized learning experiences through adaptive learning platforms that adjust to each student's comprehension level and learning pace.

4.5 Assessing Differentiated Learning Outcomes in Indian Schools

Evaluating the outcomes of differentiated instruction in Indian schools is essential to ensure that personalized and adaptive teaching methods effectively meet the diverse needs of each student. Unlike traditional assessments, which often depend on standardized tests, differentiated assessments evaluate students based on their individual learning paths, strengths, and needs. This is particularly critical in India's varied classroom landscapes, where students come from diverse academic, linguistic, and socio-economic backgrounds. Aligning assessments with differentiated instruction allows teachers to gain a more comprehensive understanding of each student's growth and development.

In a differentiated classroom, assessment methods vary to accommodate different ways of understanding, skills, and progress. For example, some students may excel in written tests, while others might better demonstrate their knowledge through presentations, projects, or practical applications. This flexibility helps students showcase their abilities in formats that resonate with their learning styles.

Formative assessments, which are integrated throughout the learning process, are crucial in measuring differentiated learning outcomes. In Indian classrooms, these might include quizzes, class discussions, peer reviews, or self-assessments that provide immediate feedback. Such tools enable teachers to monitor progress continuously and tailor their teaching strategies to meet student needs promptly. For instance, additional support can be provided quickly if a student is struggling with a specific concept, ensuring that no student falls behind.

Summative assessments, which occur at the end of a learning unit or term, can also be adapted for differentiated instruction. Instead of relying solely on traditional exams, teachers might employ various formats such as essays, visual timelines, or presentations in a history class to assess students' understanding of historical events. This method allows students multiple avenues to express their knowledge and skills, ensuring assessments reflect their actual learning journeys rather than just their test-taking abilities.

A significant benefit of differentiated assessment in Indian schools is its support of a growth mindset among students. By focusing on individual progress and less on peer comparison, students are encouraged to engage more deeply with their learning objectives, fostering a supportive and inclusive educational environment. This is especially valuable in classrooms with students from varied backgrounds, where it is crucial that all students feel valued for their unique contributions.

The National Education Policy (NEP) 2020 promotes a shift from rote memorization and standardized testing towards competency-based assessments that gauge genuine understanding and skills. Differentiated assessments are well-aligned with this vision, focusing on students' ability to apply their knowledge in meaningful ways. For example, in science classes, assessments might involve students designing and conducting experiments, which better reflect their critical thinking and problem-solving skills, key competencies for the 21st century.

Differentiated assessment also enhances collaboration and peer learning. In Indian classrooms, where group projects and peer evaluations are common, assessments can include evaluating how effectively students collaborate, communicate, and contribute to group tasks. These assessments not only track academic progress but also help students develop essential social and interpersonal skills.

Technology further facilitates differentiated assessments in Indian schools.

Digital tools like learning management systems (LMS) and educational apps allow teachers to create personalized assessments and provide real-time feedback, accommodating various learning styles. Data analytics offered by these tools helps teachers identify performance patterns, enabling them to make targeted adjustments to their teaching strategies.

4.6 Inclusive Education and Special Needs in India

Inclusive education, which aims to provide equal learning opportunities for all students, is particularly crucial in India due to the diversity of student needs across physical, intellectual, social, emotional, and linguistic spectrums. The National Education Policy (NEP) 2020 emphasizes the importance of this approach, advocating for the integration of all students, including those with special needs, into mainstream educational settings where they can access the same learning opportunities as their peers. Differentiated instruction plays a pivotal role in this model by adapting teaching methods to meet the varied needs of students.

Historically, students with special needs in India have encountered numerous obstacles in accessing quality education. Many schools are not equipped with the necessary infrastructure to support students with physical or cognitive disabilities. Additionally, there is often a lack of specialized resources, such as trained staff and adaptive technologies, which are critical for facilitating an inclusive learning environment. In response, inclusive education strives to remove these barriers by designing classrooms that enable all students to participate fully in learning activities. This approach may require adjustments to the curriculum, alterations to the physical layout of classrooms, and the adoption of specific teaching strategies tailored to ensure that students with special needs are accommodated effectively alongside their peers (Figure 4.3).

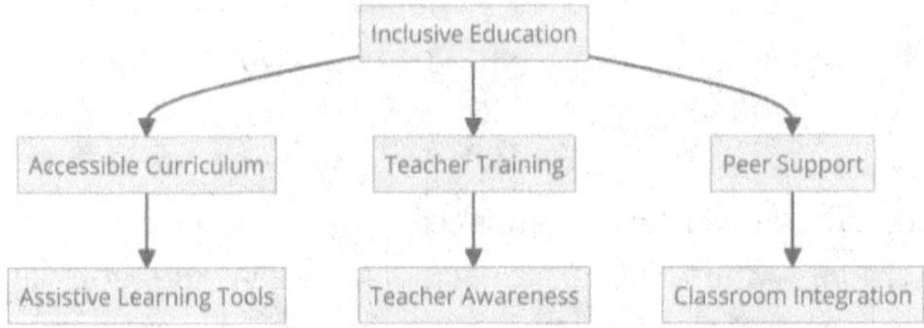

Figure 4.3: This diagram illustrates the **Role of Inclusive Education in Supporting Students with Special Needs in Indian Schools**:

- **Inclusive Education**:
  o Focuses on providing equal educational opportunities for all students,

including those with special needs.

- **Accessible Curriculum**:
  - o Ensures that the curriculum is adaptable to all students.
  - o Includes the use of **Assistive Learning Tools** to support students with special needs.
- **Teacher Training**:
  - o Involves training educators to understand and support special needs students.
  - o Includes **Teacher Awareness** programs to ensure inclusive teaching practices.
- **Peer Support**:
  - o Encourages collaboration and integration of students with special needs into regular classrooms.
  - o Promotes **Classroom Integration** to foster inclusion in learning environments.

One of the fundamental tenets of inclusive education is that all students, regardless of their specific needs or abilities, should be educated in an environment that is supportive and nurturing. For students with special needs, this often involves differentiated instruction, where teaching methods and lessons are customized to meet individual learning styles and capabilities. For instance, students with hearing impairments may benefit from visual aids and written directions, while those with learning disabilities might need additional time for assignments or access to assistive technologies. Such accommodations help ensure that students with special needs can fully engage with educational content and achieve success.

The National Education Policy (NEP) 2020 underscores the importance of inclusive schools, promoting the principles of Universal Design for Learning (UDL). UDL calls for flexible learning environments that can accommodate the varied needs of all students. It supports the use of diverse methods for representation, engagement, and expression, aligning with the objectives of differentiated instruction to make education accessible and beneficial for every student, regardless of ability.

Technology plays a crucial role in facilitating inclusive education. Assistive technologies like screen readers, text-to-speech software, and interactive whiteboards enable students with disabilities to access educational materials and participate fully in classroom activities. For example, a visually impaired student might use a screen reader to access digital textbooks, while a student with dyslexia could benefit from text-to-speech software to aid in reading assignments. These technologies allow students with special needs to integrate more seamlessly into mainstream classrooms, promoting inclusivity.

In rural areas of India, where specialized resources may be scarce, inclusive education can still be effectively implemented using innovative, low-cost methods. Teachers can create tactile learning tools from locally available materials for visually impaired students or modify classroom activities to accommodate students with physical disabilities. Peer support plays a vital role in these settings, fostering a cooperative learning environment where students assist one another, ensuring that those with special needs are integrated into group activities and discussions.

Teacher training is critical for the success of inclusive education. Many educators in India may lack the necessary training to adequately support students with special needs, which can hinder the adoption of inclusive practices. The NEP 2020 emphasizes the importance of ongoing professional development, focusing on equipping teachers with the skills to adapt curriculum, utilize assistive technologies, and cultivate supportive classroom environments for all students.

4.7 Teacher Training for Differentiated Instruction in India

Teacher training is crucial for the effective implementation of differentiated instruction in Indian classrooms. Differentiated instruction involves adopting flexible teaching strategies tailored to the diverse learning needs of students. In India, where classrooms typically comprise students with varied academic abilities, learning styles, linguistic backgrounds, and socio-economic conditions, it is essential that teachers possess the skills to customize their lessons to meet each student's individual needs. The National Education Policy (NEP) 2020 emphasizes the importance of professional development for teachers, particularly in the realm of differentiated and inclusive teaching practices, to ensure educators can deliver personalized learning experiences effectively.

Differentiated instruction marks a departure from traditional, uniform teaching approaches, moving towards dynamic, student-centered methods. This transition can pose challenges, especially for teachers accustomed to more conventional educational methods. Thus, professional development programs focusing on differentiated instruction are vital. These programs start by aiding educators in recognizing the diverse needs of their students, such as differences in academic readiness, learning preferences, interests, and cultural backgrounds. Training teachers to identify and understand these differences lays the groundwork for designing lessons that address the unique requirements of each student. For example, while visual learners might benefit more from diagrams and charts, auditory learners might find discussions and lectures more effective.

A critical component of teacher training for differentiated instruction involves learning to design flexible lesson plans. Educators need guidance on creating tiered assignments, scaffolded activities, and assessments that cater to students' varying levels of understanding and pace. In a mathematics class, for instance, a teacher might develop tasks of differing complexities, allowing advanced students to tackle more challenging problems, while providing foundational tasks to those who need more support. Such tiered instruction ensures that all students face appropriate challenges without feeling overwhelmed or disengaged.

Moreover, teacher training must cover the use of diverse instructional strategies to cater to different learning styles. This might include integrating visual aids, hands-on activities, group work, and technology into lessons. For instance, digital simulations might help visual learners in a science class understand complex concepts, whereas kinesthetic learners might benefit from participating in laboratory experiments. Diverse teaching methods ensure that all students engage with the material in a way that best suits their learning style.

Technology is integral to supporting differentiated instruction, and teacher training programs should focus on how educators can effectively integrate digital tools into their teaching practices. E-learning platforms and digital tools can provide personalized learning experiences, featuring adaptive quizzes, multimedia resources, and interactive content that students can explore at their own pace. Teachers must be trained to leverage these tools effectively to enhance their teaching and offer customized learning opportunities. Platforms like SWAYAM and DIKSHA, which provide free online courses and resources, are invaluable for teachers looking to refine their skills in differentiated instruction.

Assessment is another crucial area in teacher training for differentiated instruction. Educators should learn to assess student progress using methods that reflect diverse learning trajectories. This might involve employing formative assessments that offer continuous feedback, as opposed to relying solely on traditional exams. Techniques such as peer reviews, self-assessments, and project-based evaluations can provide a more comprehensive view of each student's progress, aligning with their strengths and learning styles, and offering a more accurate reflection of their understanding.

The NEP 2020 advocates for ongoing professional development for teachers through workshops, seminars, and online training programs to ensure they are equipped with modern teaching strategies. Programs like NISHTHA (National Initiative for School Heads' and Teachers' Holistic Advancement) are structured to assist teachers in developing their abilities in differentiated instruction and inclusive education, focusing on creating learner-centered classrooms where all students can succeed, regardless of their backgrounds or abilities.

In rural areas, where resources and access to technology may be limited, teacher training in differentiated instruction is even more critical. Teachers facing large class sizes and inadequate infrastructure must be equipped with strategies to implement differentiated instruction using locally available materials and low-cost methods. Training programs should also help rural teachers integrate technology into their teaching, even in settings with limited resources, to support personalized learning effectively.

4.8 Successful Case Studies of Differentiated Learning in Indian Schools

Differentiated instruction has significantly impacted Indian classrooms, particularly in schools adopting flexible and inclusive teaching strategies to accommodate diverse learning needs. Numerous case studies across India illustrate how this approach enables teachers to craft engaging, personalized educational experiences, leading to notable improvements in academic outcomes. These successes underscore the influence of the National Education Policy (NEP) 2020, which advocates for innovative, student-centered learning methods.

One effective example of differentiated instruction is the incorporation of project-based learning (PBL) in some Indian schools. This method allows students to undertake projects at their own pace and in styles that best suit their learning preferences. For instance, in a Delhi school, a social studies class tasked students with exploring and presenting various global cultures. Choices ranged from multimedia presentations to art projects and written reports, enabling students to express their understanding in ways that leveraged their individual strengths, thereby boosting creativity and engagement.

In Maharashtra, a government school has successfully implemented tiered assignments within its mathematics curriculum to address different levels of student proficiency. Students with a stronger grasp of math engaged in complex problem-solving to challenge their critical thinking skills, while others worked on simpler, foundational tasks, ensuring personalized progression and sustained engagement, which enhanced overall academic performance.

In rural Rajasthan, where resources are often scarce, differentiated instruction has tailored teaching methods to local conditions. Teachers have utilized local materials for hands-on science education, moving beyond textbook reliance to engage students in building simple machines or studying local flora and fauna. This practical approach has made science more relatable and accessible, particularly benefiting students who find traditional text-based learning challenging.

Technology also plays a pivotal role in facilitating differentiated instruction. For example, an urban school in Bengaluru has integrated digital learning platforms that provide adaptive learning experiences. This technology customizes tasks to student abilities, offers immediate feedback, and adjusts difficulty based on individual performance, significantly enhancing student engagement and academic results.

In Chennai, peer tutoring has been implemented to support students of varying abilities. Older or more advanced students mentor their younger or less proficient peers, particularly in challenging subjects like mathematics and science. This method has not only bolstered the academic outcomes of the mentees but also developed the tutors' leadership and communication skills, demonstrating that differentiated instruction can be effectively implemented even without advanced technology.

These case studies align with the NEP 2020's goals, which promote flexible, personalized, and inclusive education. By moving away from rote learning and standardized teaching, these schools foster environments that encourage critical thinking, collaboration, and exploration in ways that resonate with each student's unique learning style. The policy's focus on experiential and skill-based learning further supports these initiatives, emphasizing the importance of real-world applications in education.

CHAPTER 5

EXPERIENTIAL AND PROJECT-BASED LEARNING

5.1 The Value of Experiential Learning in India

Experiential learning, which emphasizes active engagement and "learning by doing," has emerged as a transformative educational strategy in India. This approach allows students to apply theoretical concepts in practical situations, enhancing their critical thinking, problem-solving abilities, and practical skills. In India, where traditional education has often centered around lectures and examinations, experiential learning represents a shift towards more dynamic and impactful learning experiences. It fosters active participation and reflective thinking, deepening students' understanding of academic subjects and equipping them with essential skills for real-world challenges.

Historically, India's educational philosophy, exemplified by the Gurukuls, has valued practical knowledge and learning through direct experience, with students developing skills under the mentorship of a guru. Today, experiential learning reinvigorates this age-old philosophy by incorporating modern techniques and technologies. Through internships, field trips, experiments, and community service projects, students gain practical experience that not only complements their academic learning but also bridges the gap between classroom education and external realities.

One of the significant benefits of experiential learning in India is its adaptability to diverse learning styles. In a country characterized by large and varied classroom settings, experiential learning provides a flexible framework that can engage students of different academic levels, socio-economic backgrounds, and personal interests. For example, a lesson on environmental conservation might involve a field trip to a forest or a river clean-up activity. This hands-on approach is particularly beneficial for students who may struggle with conventional textbook learning, allowing them to interact with the material in a more engaging and tangible manner. By offering multiple points of entry into a topic, experiential learning ensures that all students have the chance to excel.

Moreover, experiential learning is crucial in cultivating essential life skills such as communication, teamwork, and leadership. In a societal context like India's, where collaboration and adaptability are highly prized, experiential learning provides early opportunities for students to develop these competencies. Activities such as group projects and community initiatives encourage students to work together, share ideas, and collectively address challenges, thereby not only reinforcing academic concepts but also preparing them for future professional environments where teamwork and interpersonal skills are key.

The National Education Policy (NEP) 2020 underscores the importance of experiential learning, advocating a shift away from rote learning towards a more holistic, skill-based approach. The policy promotes the integration of experiential learning at all educational levels, transforming students from passive recipients of information to active participants in their educational journeys. By championing experiential learning, the NEP 2020 aims to align education more closely with students' needs and prepare them for the demands of the contemporary workforce (Figure 5.1).

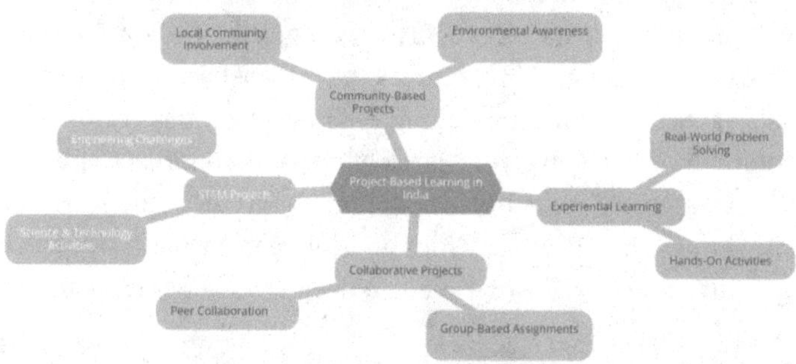

Figure 5.1: This mind map showcases examples of **Experiential and Project-Based Learning** in Indian classrooms:

- **Experiential Learning**:
o Focuses on real-world problem-solving and hands-on activities.
- **Collaborative Projects**:
o Involves group-based assignments and peer collaboration.
- **STEM Projects**:
o Includes activities related to science, technology, and engineering challenges.
- **Community-Based Projects**:
o Encourages local community involvement and environmental awareness.

Experiential learning has significantly influenced vocational education in India, particularly in sectors where practical, hands-on experience is paramount. Vocational training programs across fields such as agriculture, manufacturing, and healthcare extensively utilize internships, apprenticeships, and on-the-job training to equip students with career-ready skills. By engaging directly with industry professionals, students not only acquire technical knowledge but also gain a comprehensive understanding of the practical realities within their chosen sectors.

In rural areas of India, experiential learning is especially crucial, effectively narrowing the gap between academic knowledge and community life. Educators in these settings tailor lessons to local contexts, enhancing the relevance and accessibility of education. For instance, students in rural schools may participate in sustainable farming projects either on school grounds or through community agricultural initiatives. Such activities not only deepen students' understanding of environmental science but also provide them with practical skills that are immediately applicable to their local environments. This method of teaching not only promotes educational attainment but also contributes to community development, aligning educational outcomes with local needs and opportunities.

5.2 Designing Effective Project-Based Lessons for Indian Students

Project-based learning (PBL) represents a transformative shift in India's educational landscape, transitioning away from traditional rote learning and examinations to a more engaging, student-centered approach. PBL immerses learners in real-world scenarios, enabling them to apply their academic knowledge through hands-on activities and collaborative problem-solving, thus fostering critical thinking, creativity, and a deeper understanding of the subject matter.

For PBL to resonate effectively with Indian students, lessons need to be culturally relevant and directly connected to their everyday lives. A critical component of PBL is the intrinsic motivation that students experience when working on projects that address real-world challenges. For instance, a project focusing on water conservation could be particularly impactful for students in areas facing water scarcity, making the learning process both relevant and urgent. By aligning projects with local issues, educators can enhance student engagement and encourage a sense of ownership over their learning.

Inquiry and exploration are fundamental to PBL. Instead of simply delivering answers, educators encourage students to pose questions, investigate problems, and devise their own solutions. In a typical scenario, students in a science class might explore methods to minimize plastic waste within their community. This could involve conducting research, engaging with local stakeholders, and proposing viable solutions. Such an inquiry-based approach not only sharpens critical thinking but also enhances skills in collaboration and problem-solving.

Collaboration is another crucial aspect of PBL. By working in groups, students have the opportunity to exchange ideas, communicate effectively, and pursue common objectives. This is especially beneficial in large Indian classrooms, where group projects can facilitate meaningful peer interactions. Collaborative efforts not only bolster academic learning but also cultivate vital life skills such as leadership, teamwork, and conflict resolution (Figure 5.2).

To maximize the benefits of PBL, it is essential for teachers to find the right balance between providing guidance and granting students the freedom to explore. While it is important to set clear expectations and deadlines, students should be given the autonomy to determine how they approach their projects. For example, a teacher might outline the goal-such as investigating a historical event or designing an eco-friendly product-while allowing students the flexibility to choose their research methods or the format for their final presentations. This blend of structured guidance with exploratory freedom not only stimulates creativity but also maintains student focus and commitment to their projects.

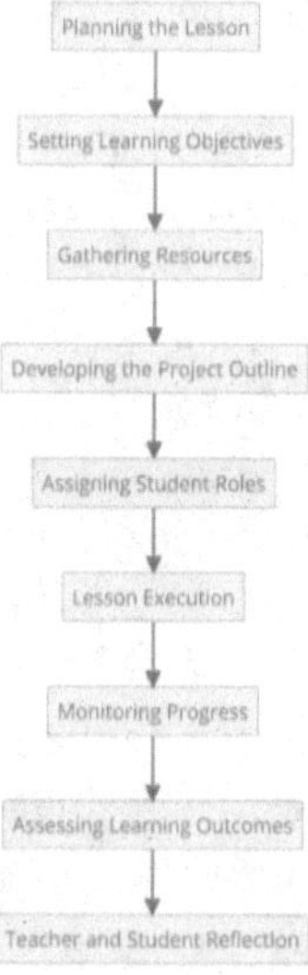

Figure 5.2: This flowchart outlines the steps for **Designing Effective Project-Based Lessons**:

1. **Planning the Lesson**: Initial step where teachers plan the overall structure.

2. **Setting Learning Objectives**: Clear goals are defined for student outcomes.

3. **Gathering Resources**: Collect necessary materials and resources.

4. **Developing the Project Outline**: Create a detailed plan for the project.

5. **Assigning Student Roles**: Distribute responsibilities among students.

6. **Lesson Execution**: Students begin working on their projects.

7. **Monitoring Progress**: Teachers track student performance.

8. **Assessing Learning Outcomes**: Evaluate the success of the project.

9. **Teacher and Student Reflection**: Both parties reflect on the learning experience.

Assessing student performance in project-based learning (PBL) necessitates a shift away from traditional evaluation methods. Rather than focusing solely on exams or written reports, teachers assess students based on their participation, problem-solving abilities, creativity, and teamwork throughout the project. In Indian classrooms, where assessments have traditionally been centered around exams, transitioning to this holistic approach poses challenges but also offers significant rewards. Teachers can utilize rubrics that not only evaluate the final project outcomes but also the learning process itself, including how effectively students collaborate, apply critical thinking, and adapt to challenges.

Technology plays a crucial role in facilitating project-based lessons in India. With digital tools, students are able to research topics, collaborate with peers through communication platforms, and present their work using multimedia formats such as videos and presentations. In urban schools, where technological infrastructure is more advanced, students can leverage these tools to delve into global issues and enhance their projects. Conversely, in rural areas where technology access may be more restricted, teachers can still orchestrate impactful project-based lessons using locally available resources. This encourages students to engage with and investigate their immediate surroundings and community.

The National Education Policy (NEP) 2020 underscores the significance of project-based and experiential learning within India's educational framework. The policy advocates for the integration of PBL into the curriculum at all educational levels, from primary through to higher secondary education. By endorsing PBL, the NEP 2020 aims to move away from rote memorization towards a more comprehensive, skill-based educational system. This approach equips students with essential skills such as critical thinking, creativity, collaboration, and problem-solving, preparing them to tackle the challenges of the 21st century.

5.3 Case Studies in Experiential Learning from Indian Schools

Experiential learning, which emphasizes hands-on experiences and reflective learning, has significantly gained traction in India, with numerous schools adopting this approach to actively engage students in applying their knowledge practically. Such methods provide students with valuable opportunities to develop critical thinking and problem-solving skills while deepening their connection to the subject matter.

A notable example of this approach is a school in Kerala that introduced a project-based environmental science curriculum focusing on local ecological issues. Students were tasked with identifying local environmental challenges such as waste management, water conservation, or deforestation, and developing practical solutions. Through fieldwork, research, and collaboration with local communities, students not only learned about the impact of these issues but also proposed sustainable solutions, enhancing their understanding of environmental science and instilling a sense of community and environmental responsibility.

In Rajasthan, a rural school initiated an agricultural education project where students managed a school garden. This project aimed to educate students about sustainable farming practices, crop cycles, and environmental conservation. Throughout the academic year, students took responsibility for planting, maintaining, and harvesting crops, which were then utilized in the school's midday meal program. This initiative not only connected students with local agricultural practices but also taught them valuable science, teamwork, and problem-solving skills, making the academic content highly relevant to their everyday lives.

In urban settings, a school in Mumbai integrated experiential learning through design thinking and entrepreneurship programs. Students were encouraged to identify real-world problems, devise innovative solutions, and develop prototypes or business models. Projects included designing cost-effective water filtration systems for slums and developing apps to promote mental health awareness. These activities not only enhanced students' critical thinking and creativity but also provided them with practical skills in business, technology, and leadership, aligning with the National Education Policy (NEP) 2020's goals of fostering entrepreneurial and life skills.

In West Bengal, another form of experiential learning involved a cultural heritage preservation project. Collaborating with local artisans, a school taught students traditional crafts such as pottery, weaving, and painting, exploring their historical and cultural significance. This project not only gave students hands-on artistic experiences but also contributed to preserving the region's cultural heritage by imparting traditional skills to the next generation, thereby fostering a connection to cultural roots and promoting pride in heritage.

5.4 Real-World Applications and Community Involvement in Indian Education

In India, integrating real-world applications and community engagement into the education system has proven effective in making learning more relevant and impactful for students. This approach connects classroom lessons with practical experiences, enabling students to actively engage with their communities, thereby deepening their understanding of academic subjects while cultivating social responsibility and civic involvement. This educational strategy is in harmony with the National Education Policy (NEP) 2020, which emphasizes the importance of experiential learning, skill development, and community participation in education.

A significant advantage of incorporating real-world applications in education is that it allows students to see the practical relevance of their studies. Traditional teaching methods in Indian schools often focus on rote memorization and textbook learning. In contrast, real-world applications provide opportunities for students to apply theoretical knowledge in practical scenarios. For example, a geometry lesson might be connected to a community project where students design and measure layouts for local parks or playgrounds. This application not only helps students understand abstract concepts more concretely but also enhances the learning experience by making it more engaging and enjoyable.

In rural areas, where many students have agricultural backgrounds, applying education to real-life contexts is particularly beneficial. Schools in these regions have incorporated agricultural education into their curricula, engaging students in farming projects that teach sustainable agriculture, crop cycles, and environmental conservation. Through participation in school farms or local agricultural initiatives, students acquire practical skills that are directly applicable to their community settings. This integration not only enriches their understanding of science and environmental studies but also equips them with valuable skills for daily life.

Community involvement is another crucial element in enriching students' educational experiences. Collaborating with local communities exposes students to real-world challenges and encourages them to contribute actively to solving these issues. For instance, some schools partner with local NGOs and government organizations to tackle pressing social problems like sanitation, water conservation, and health awareness. Students might engage in organizing awareness campaigns, conducting community surveys, or participating in local development projects. These activities allow students to apply their academic knowledge while developing critical life skills such as teamwork, leadership, and communication. Through such initiatives, schools not only enhance academic learning but also foster a sense of civic duty and social responsibility among students, aligning with the goals of NEP 2020 to create a more engaged, skilled, and conscientious student body.

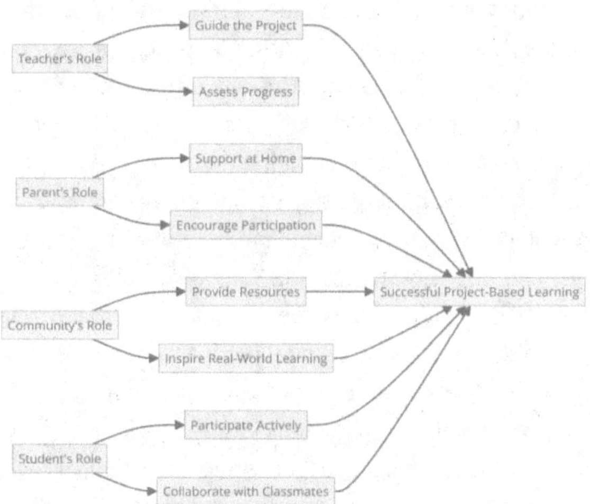

Figure 5.3: This diagram shows the roles of **Teachers, Parents, and Students** in successful project-based learning:

- **Teacher's Role**:
  o Provide project guidance and assess student work.
- **Parent's Role**:
  o Offer support and resources, and encourage student engagement.
- **Student's Role**:
  o Actively participate and collaborate with peers.
- All these roles contribute to **Successful Project-Based Learning**.

In Tamil Nadu, a school launched a water conservation initiative in collaboration with local authorities, providing a compelling example of effective community involvement in education. Students participated in surveys to assess water usage within their village and led awareness campaigns to promote water-saving practices. They also worked with local farmers to implement rainwater harvesting systems. This hands-on project allowed students to utilize their scientific knowledge to tackle a critical community issue, fostering a sense of ownership and responsibility that enriched their educational experience.

In urban areas, schools have embraced real-world applications in subjects like entrepreneurship and social studies. For example, students in various cities undertake business simulation projects, creating mock companies, developing products, and pitching their business ideas to potential investors. These activities not only teach economic and business management concepts but also provide practical experience in problem-solving, negotiation, and creative thinking. Local entrepreneurs and business leaders are often invited to mentor students, strengthening the link between education and the professional world and illustrating how academic studies can translate into career opportunities.

Technology plays a pivotal role in broadening the scope of real-world applications within Indian education. Digital tools enable students to take virtual field trips, collaborate on online platforms, and engage in international projects addressing global issues like climate change, global health, or technological innovation. For instance, Indian students can collaborate with peers abroad on these projects, utilizing online tools for communication and research sharing. These experiences not only foster a global perspective but also allow students to apply their learning to significant contemporary challenges.

Additionally, real-world applications and community involvement are instrumental in cultivating social responsibility and ethical awareness among students. By participating in community-focused projects, students gain insights into the social and environmental challenges affecting their localities and are encouraged to think critically about their roles in driving meaningful change. This approach enhances civic engagement and supports the development of students into proactive, informed citizens. In a country like India, where many communities face substantial social and economic issues, engaging students in community-based projects serves as a powerful method to inspire future leaders and innovators.

The National Education Policy (NEP) 2020 strongly supports integrating community involvement and real-world applications into school curricula, advocating for a more holistic and skill-based learning approach. It emphasizes experiential learning that bridges classroom education with practical life scenarios, preparing students not only for the workforce but also instilling values like empathy, social responsibility, and environmental stewardship. This policy framework aims to transform education in India, making it more relevant, engaging, and impactful for students.

5.5 Evaluating Project-Based Learning in India

Evaluating the effectiveness of project-based learning (PBL) in India necessitates a departure from traditional assessment methods toward more comprehensive approaches that assess students' problem-solving abilities, creativity, collaboration, and practical knowledge application. In Indian education, where examinations have predominantly been the evaluation standard, PBL introduces an opportunity to assess students based on their learning journey rather than solely on the outcome. This shift emphasizes understanding student approaches and engagements in projects, providing deeper insights into their skills and growth. This approach is in line with the National Education Policy (NEP) 2020, which supports a transition from rote memorization to competency-based learning and assessments.

A critical element in evaluating PBL is the adoption of formative assessments, which offer continuous feedback throughout a project. Unlike traditional summative assessments that occur at the end of a learning period, formative assessments allow for ongoing monitoring of student progress, providing timely guidance. For instance, in a science project focusing on renewable energy, teachers might evaluate students during various project phases like research, hypothesis formulation, and prototype development. Regular feedback at these stages helps ensure that students remain aligned with project objectives, allowing for adjustments before final submissions. This method fosters a learning environment where students can iteratively refine their work, enhancing their understanding and mastery of the subject.

Rubrics are frequently utilized in PBL evaluations, offering a structured framework to assess different student performance aspects, such as creativity, teamwork, critical thinking, and the overall quality of the final product. In the context of Indian classrooms, rubrics help to standardize evaluations while accommodating diverse student demonstrations of learning. For example, in a history project requiring a presentation on a significant event, the rubric could measure the thoroughness of research, effectiveness of collaboration, clarity of communication, and the depth and accuracy of content.

Peer and self-assessments also play vital roles in PBL evaluations. Group projects, for instance, can benefit from peer assessments where students evaluate both their contributions and those of their peers, offering insights into group dynamics and individual participation. This method encourages students to reflect on their learning processes, recognize team strengths and weaknesses, and appreciate the value of effective collaboration. In Indian classrooms, where collaborative activities are increasingly emphasized, peer evaluations promote a culture of mutual responsibility and collective learning.

Self-assessment is equally critical, encouraging students to take ownership of their learning. Through self-evaluation, students can gauge their progress, identify areas needing improvement, and set objectives for future projects. This practice is particularly transformative in Indian educational settings traditionally dominated by teacher-led instructions, as it fosters student autonomy and self-regulation. Reflecting on their performances allows students to become more self-aware and accountable, aligning with NEP 2020's goals.

5.6 Using Local Resources for Experiential Learning in India

One highly effective method to implement experiential learning in Indian schools is by leveraging local resources to craft practical, hands-on educational experiences. Utilizing the natural environment, cultural practices, historical landmarks, and community expertise provides ample opportunities for students to engage deeply with their surroundings, anchoring abstract concepts in real-world contexts they understand well. The National Education Policy (NEP) 2020 champions this approach, advocating for education that is contextualized and skill-based, aiming to enhance critical thinking, problem-solving abilities, and a comprehensive understanding of academic subjects.

In rural areas, where access to modern educational tools might be restricted, local resources are especially crucial for facilitating experiential learning. For instance, schools in agricultural zones might integrate farming practices into their science and environmental studies curricula. This allows students to explore plant biology, soil science, and sustainable farming methods firsthand through activities in school gardens or local farming projects. Such direct involvement not only enriches their scientific knowledge but also equips them with practical skills pertinent to their local environment.

Similarly, local ecosystems are a treasure trove for experiential learning across both rural and urban settings. Schools situated near rivers, forests, or mountains might organize field trips for students to study local wildlife, investigate environmental issues like pollution or deforestation, and participate in conservation initiatives. In coastal regions, such as Tamil Nadu or Kerala, students might engage in beach clean-up activities, enhancing their understanding of marine ecosystems and the human impact on these habitats, fostering a sense of environmental stewardship.

In urban contexts, local historical sites, museums, and industries provide valuable learning experiences. Schools in cities like Delhi, Mumbai, and Kolkata often facilitate visits to significant cultural landmarks, where students can connect with the region's history and culture firsthand. Experiencing historical sites like the Qutub Minar or the Red Fort firsthand brings history to life, enabling students to appreciate the architecture and stories beyond textbook narratives. Visits to local industries also offer insights into engineering, economics, and production processes, linking classroom learning to real-world applications.

Local artisans and craftspeople also play a crucial role in experiential learning by bringing traditional crafts such as weaving, pottery, and metalworking into the classroom. By inviting artisans to demonstrate their crafts, students not only learn these skills hands-on but also help preserve and appreciate their cultural heritage. For instance, students in Gujarat might learn Bandhani, a traditional tie-dye technique, from local experts, gaining both practical skills and cultural insights.

5.7 Role of NGOs in Supporting Experiential Learning in India

In India, non-governmental organizations (NGOs) play a vital role in enhancing experiential learning, particularly in regions where educational resources are scarce. By forming partnerships with schools and local communities, NGOs help bridge the gap between traditional curricula and the practical, hands-on educational experiences that are crucial for comprehensive learning. This collaborative approach is in line with the directives of the National Education Policy (NEP) 2020, which advocates for integrating real-world skills and problem-solving into educational frameworks to prepare students for future challenges.

NGOs contribute significantly by providing access to resources and expertise that might be unavailable in under-resourced schools. Many of these organizations specialize in fields such as environmental science, social justice, health, and vocational training, offering students opportunities to engage in relevant, hands-on activities. For example, environmental NGOs may facilitate tree-planting campaigns or biodiversity studies, enabling students to explore ecological concepts actively and contextually. These activities not only deepen understanding but also instill a sense of environmental responsibility.

In rural India, the impact of NGOs is particularly pronounced. Organizations like Pratham have implemented numerous initiatives aimed at improving educational outcomes by integrating local issues such as sanitation, water conservation, and health awareness into learning projects. These initiatives allow students to apply theoretical knowledge in practical settings, thereby enhancing the educational experience and making it more relevant to students' lives.

The Barefoot College in Rajasthan is a prime example of an NGO that fosters experiential learning through programs that impart practical skills like solar engineering and sustainable agriculture. These programs are designed not just to educate but to empower students, equipping them with the skills needed to address and solve local challenges.

In urban areas, NGOs often work with schools to introduce experiential learning projects focused on social justice and civic engagement. For instance, collaborations with organizations like Teach For India help develop project-based learning initiatives that tackle issues such as gender equality and economic disparity. These projects encourage students to actively engage with their communities, promoting a deeper connection with the content and developing essential skills such as leadership and empathy.

Moreover, NGOs play a crucial role in vocational education by providing job-related training through practical, hands-on experiences. For example, organizations like the Smile Foundation and the Aga Khan Foundation offer programs in healthcare, IT, and entrepreneurship, often including internships or apprenticeships that enhance the bridge between education and employment.

NGOs also support teacher development by offering training programs that help educators incorporate project-based and experiential learning into their classrooms. This training is essential for teachers to effectively facilitate and guide hands-on learning experiences. Additionally, NGOs help forge connections between schools and a broader community of local experts, artisans, and businesses, enriching the educational ecosystem and providing students with access to a diverse range of real-world experiences and mentorships.

5.8 Teacher-Parent Collaboration in Experiential Learning Projects

Teacher-parent collaboration is an essential component in the successful implementation of experiential learning projects in Indian schools. This partnership enhances the learning environment by extending supportive resources beyond the classroom, which is critical for grounding academic concepts in real-world applications. The National Education Policy (NEP) 2020 emphasizes the importance of parent involvement in creating a holistic, skill-based educational approach.

Experiential learning often necessitates activities outside the traditional classroom setting, such as fieldwork, community involvement, or practical experiments. In these scenarios, parental support is crucial for facilitating student engagement and providing the necessary resources and motivation. For example, in a project where students are tasked with growing plants at home, parent involvement might include helping to secure gardening supplies, overseeing the project's progress, and offering encouragement. This active engagement not only bolsters the educational experience but also provides a platform for parents to actively participate in their child's educational journey.

Teachers in many Indian schools report that students whose parents are engaged in their experiential learning projects tend to show improved performance and greater enthusiasm towards their studies. Parental involvement is particularly valuable in project-based learning where projects often require tasks to be completed outside of school hours. For instance, parents can aid in community survey projects by facilitating access to the community, providing insights, or assisting with data collection. This collaborative effort effectively bridges classroom learning and real-life applications, making the educational process more relevant and impactful for students.

Effective communication between teachers and parents is vital for fostering this collaborative relationship. Regular updates on the student's progress, project goals, and opportunities for home support are essential. Communication can occur through various channels such as parent-teacher meetings, progress reports, or informal interactions during school events. Prior to initiating a project, such as one focusing on local environmental conservation, teachers might hold meetings with parents to discuss the project's objectives, expected roles, and required resources. Engaging parents from the outset helps to align home support with the educational activities at school.

Advancements in technology have further facilitated teacher-parent collaboration on experiential learning projects. Digital tools like school apps or messaging platforms enable teachers to share updates, feedback, and communicate directly with parents about their child's progress. In urban areas with better access to technology, these tools keep parents well-informed about their children's assignments and support needs. Even in rural settings, where digital access may be more limited, regular in-person meetings and clear communication strategies ensure that parents are engaged and informed about project expectations and timelines.

Parental involvement also plays a critical role in ensuring safety during experiential learning activities that involve field trips or community interactions. For projects that include visits to local historical sites or community clean-up initiatives, parents often assist by accompanying students and helping supervise activities.

CHAPTER 6

CULTURALLY RESPONSIVE TEACHING

6.1 Importance of Cultural Awareness in Indian Education

Culturally responsive teaching in India encompasses an understanding and appreciation of the diverse cultural backgrounds of students, using this awareness to inform and adapt teaching methods, curricula, and the overall learning environment. Given India's vast cultural diversity, which includes a myriad of languages, religions, traditions, and socioeconomic backgrounds, it's crucial to embed cultural awareness in educational practices. This approach enables the creation of inclusive and engaging learning experiences that resonate deeply with students from all cultural milieus.

A fundamental aspect of culturally responsive teaching is linguistic diversity recognition. In many classrooms across India, students come from homes where regional languages prevail, often different from the instructional language at school. Culturally responsive educators address this by employing bilingual resources, allowing student expression in native languages, and integrating local dialects into lessons. The National Education Policy (NEP) 2020 supports this through its advocacy for multilingual education and the use of the mother tongue as the medium of instruction during the early educational years, enhancing both comprehension and learning outcomes.

Additionally, respecting and understanding religious and social diversity is paramount. India's plethora of religious and cultural traditions means that students often bring varied religious practices and values into the classroom. Educators must navigate these differences with sensitivity, ensuring that teaching materials and classroom interactions respect diverse religious and cultural practices. For instance, discussions around festivals, historical events, or social customs should present balanced perspectives that acknowledge all communities, fostering an inclusive environment that promotes mutual respect among students.

Socioeconomic diversity is another critical factor in culturally responsive teaching. With significant economic disparities affecting access to education and resources in India, it is vital for educators to understand and address the challenges faced by students from less privileged backgrounds. This might involve adapting classroom activities and assignments to ensure no student is excluded due to a lack of resources, such as internet access or educational materials, providing equitable learning opportunities for all.

Integrating indigenous knowledge and local traditions into the curriculum also plays a crucial role in culturally responsive teaching. India's indigenous communities hold extensive knowledge in areas such as agriculture, medicine, ecology, and crafts, which can enrich subjects like science, social studies, and environmental education. By incorporating this indigenous knowledge, educational practices not only validate these cultural contributions but also enhance students' understanding of these fields.

Moreover, culturally responsive teaching enhances the relevance of educational content by linking lessons to the students' cultural experiences. For example, a geography lesson on climate impact on agriculture can incorporate examples from the students' local regions to illustrate how local farming practices are influenced by climate. This method not only makes the learning more relatable and meaningful but also encourages students to apply their knowledge practically.

Such teaching approaches also foster empathy and cross-cultural understanding, preparing students to thrive in a multicultural society. Teachers can facilitate this by creating opportunities for students to explore and learn about different cultural backgrounds through discussions, collaborative projects, and cultural exchange activities.

6.2 Strategies for Culturally Responsive Teaching in Indian Classrooms

Culturally responsive pedagogy within Indian educational settings encompasses methodologies that recognize and honor student diversity, ensuring each learner feels appreciated and comprehended. Considering India's extensive cultural, linguistic, and socio-economic variations, educators must adopt adaptable and inclusive approaches to cultivate an atmosphere where every student can thrive. This methodology not only improves educational outcomes but also nurtures empathy, respect, and cohesion among pupils. The National Education Policy (NEP) 2020 underscores the significance of culturally responsive teaching, highlighting the necessity for an educational framework that is more inclusive and honors India's multifaceted cultural landscape.

A prominent tactic for implementing culturally responsive teaching is the adoption of multilingual instruction. Given that students in Indian classrooms frequently originate from diverse linguistic backgrounds, the use of multiple languages facilitates the bridging of communication barriers and enhances accessibility to learning. For example, educators can incorporate students' native languages alongside the primary medium of instruction to elucidate complex ideas or provide directions. This method assists learners who may face challenges with the dominant language medium, making them feel more comfortable and self-assured in their academic pursuits. The NEP 2020 endorses this approach by promoting mother tongue education, especially during the early years of schooling, to bolster understanding and engagement.

Additionally, integrating culturally pertinent content into the curriculum serves as another essential strategy. Educators can embed examples, narratives, and case studies derived from the students' own cultural contexts to render learning more significant and relatable. For instance, in history classes, an instructor might include regional historical events or notable figures from the students' areas, thereby facilitating a deeper connection with the subject matter. Similarly, in literature courses, incorporating works from local authors or folklore allows students to see their own cultural heritage reflected in their studies. This strategy not only enhances the engagement level of lessons but also instills a sense of pride in students' cultural identities (Figure 6.1).

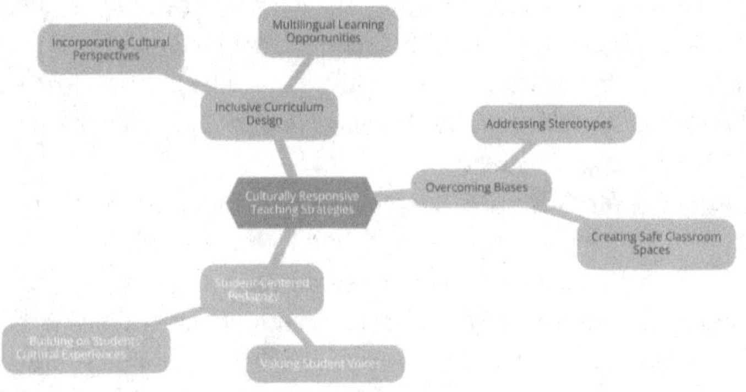

Figure 6.1: This mind map illustrates strategies for **Culturally Responsive Teaching**:

- **Inclusive Curriculum Design**:
  o Incorporating cultural perspectives into lessons.
  o Offering multilingual learning opportunities.
- **Overcoming Biases**:
  o Addressing stereotypes in the classroom.
  o Creating safe spaces for all students.
- **Student-Centered Pedagogy**:
  o Valuing student voices.

Building on students' cultural experiences.

Educators can modify their instructional approaches to accommodate diverse cultural learning preferences. In certain cultures, students are more accustomed to collective or cooperative learning environments, where group collaboration and teamwork take precedence over individual accomplishments. By integrating group activities, peer teaching, and collaborative projects, instructors can cultivate a learning atmosphere that mirrors these cultural values. For example, in classrooms comprising students from rural backgrounds, where communal living and collective efforts are prevalent, teachers might design group assignments that require students to collaborate in problem-solving or task completion. This methodology not only aligns with students' cultural experiences but also promotes the development of teamwork and communication skills.

Establishing robust relationships with students and gaining insight into their cultural backgrounds constitutes another pivotal strategy in culturally responsive teaching. Educators can endeavor to understand students' family traditions, festivals, and community practices, thereby incorporating these elements into classroom interactions. For instance, during celebrations such as Diwali, Eid, or Pongal, teachers can encourage students to share their personal experiences of these festivals, fostering an inclusive classroom environment that honors diversity. When students perceive that their cultural experiences are acknowledged and respected, they are more inclined to engage actively in classroom activities.

Beyond appreciating cultural backgrounds, it is essential for educators to remain cognizant of socio-economic disparities within Indian classrooms. In numerous schools, particularly government institutions, there exists a significant gap between students from affluent families and those from economically disadvantaged backgrounds. Culturally responsive teachers recognize these disparities and ensure that educational activities do not marginalize students who may lack access to resources at home. For example, rather than assigning homework that necessitates internet access, teachers can offer in-class activities or alternative assignments for students with limited resources. This approach guarantees that all students, irrespective of their socio-economic status, have an equitable opportunity to succeed.

Employing culturally relevant assessment methods is another critical strategy. Standardized tests may not accurately capture the abilities of students from diverse cultural or linguistic backgrounds. Culturally responsive educators can utilize a variety of assessment tools, such as oral presentations, group projects, or creative assignments, allowing students to demonstrate their understanding in ways that resonate with their cultural experiences. For instance, in a classroom with a multitude of linguistic backgrounds, teachers might permit students to explain concepts in their native languages or incorporate culturally pertinent examples in their work. This flexibility in assessment ensures that all students have a fair chance to showcase their knowledge and skills.

Ongoing professional development and teacher training are essential for the effective implementation of culturally responsive teaching strategies. Educators require continuous training to adapt their instructional methods to the cultural and linguistic diversity of their students. Workshops, seminars, and collaborative peer interactions can assist teachers in acquiring best practices for integrating cultural awareness into their teaching. The National Education Policy (NEP) 2020 underscores the importance of sustained teacher education, particularly in inclusive and culturally responsive teaching, to ensure that educators are well-equipped to address the needs of diverse student populations.

Incorporating local culture and indigenous knowledge systems into the curriculum represents another potent strategy. India is rich in traditional knowledge, especially in areas such as agriculture, medicine, and environmental conservation. Educators can leverage this knowledge by inviting local experts or community elders to share their experiences with students or organizing field trips to local farms, historical sites, or cultural centers. For example, in a science lesson on medicinal plants, teachers might invite a local herbalist to discuss traditional remedies, providing students with a practical understanding of the subject matter. This approach not only enriches the curriculum but also acknowledges the importance of indigenous knowledge in contemporary education.

Creating an inclusive classroom environment is fundamental to culturally responsive teaching. Educators can facilitate open discussions about cultural differences and promote respect for diversity through various classroom activities. For instance, students might be tasked with creating projects or presentations about their cultural heritage, which they can then share with their peers. This practice fosters cross-cultural understanding and helps students appreciate the diversity among their classmates. Additionally, teachers can establish classroom norms that emphasize mutual respect, kindness, and empathy, thereby creating a safe space where students feel comfortable expressing themselves.

6.3 Inclusive Curriculum Design for India's Multicultural Society

Designing an inclusive curriculum within India's multicultural landscape is crucial for providing students from diverse cultural, linguistic, and socio-economic backgrounds with a meaningful and equitable education. India's classrooms, characterized by a rich tapestry of languages, religions, and regional traditions, embody a wide array of experiences and perspectives. An inclusive curriculum embraces this diversity by offering content and pedagogical approaches tailored to the unique needs and backgrounds of each student. This fosters a more engaging, relevant, and respectful learning environment, aligning with the objectives outlined in the National Education Policy (NEP) 2020.

A fundamental principle of inclusive curriculum design is the representation of India's diverse student population in learning materials and content. This involves moving beyond a singular, standardized narrative to include stories, examples, and case studies from various cultural, linguistic, and regional contexts. For instance, history lessons within an inclusive curriculum would not only address national events but also highlight contributions from different regions, communities, and marginalized groups. In literature classes, students might engage with works by a wide range of Indian authors, encompassing different languages and cultural backgrounds. This approach allows students from all backgrounds to see themselves reflected in their education, thereby enhancing their sense of belonging and engagement.

Accommodating the linguistic diversity of Indian students is another critical aspect of inclusive curriculum design. With hundreds of languages spoken across the country, many students come from households where regional languages or dialects are predominant. While the medium of instruction may vary, an inclusive curriculum ensures that learning materials are accessible in students' mother tongues, particularly during the foundational years of education. The NEP 2020 strongly advocates for the use of the mother tongue as the primary medium of instruction in early education, recognizing that children learn most effectively in the language spoken at home. By incorporating bilingual or multilingual resources, schools can support students as they transition from their home language to the school language, preserving their linguistic and cultural identities.

Integrating local knowledge and traditions into the curriculum is another vital component of an inclusive educational framework. Indigenous communities, along with rural and regional populations in India, possess rich knowledge systems related to agriculture, medicine, craftsmanship, and ecology. Incorporating these knowledge systems into the curriculum not only deepens students' understanding but also validates the cultural contributions of these communities. For example, a science curriculum might include lessons on traditional farming practices or herbal medicine, allowing students to learn from their cultural heritage. This approach bridges the gap between modern education and indigenous knowledge, fostering respect for traditional wisdom.

Addressing socio-economic disparities is also essential in the design of an inclusive curriculum. In many Indian classrooms, particularly in government schools, there is a pronounced disparity between students from affluent families and those from economically disadvantaged backgrounds. An inclusive curriculum ensures that all students, regardless of their socio-economic status, have equal access to education. This might involve providing free or low-cost learning materials, designing technology-based assignments that do not require internet access, or incorporating project-based learning that avoids the need for expensive resources. By addressing these factors, schools can create a more equitable learning environment where every student has the opportunity to succeed.

Inclusivity within the curriculum extends to students with special needs as well. The NEP 2020 emphasizes the importance of inclusive education for children with disabilities, ensuring that the curriculum is adapted to meet their specific learning requirements. This can include the use of assistive technologies, alternative assessment methods, and tailored learning materials that accommodate different abilities. An inclusive curriculum allows students with disabilities to participate fully alongside their peers, fostering a sense of equality and belonging. For example, visually impaired students might use screen-reading software to access digital textbooks, or students with learning difficulties may be granted additional time to complete assignments.

Fostering cross-cultural understanding is another significant element of inclusive curriculum design. In India's multicultural society, it is imperative for students to learn to respect and appreciate the diversity of their peers. An inclusive curriculum promotes this by encouraging discussions about cultural differences, organizing cultural exchange activities, and incorporating lessons on empathy, respect, and social harmony. For instance, a social studies lesson might explore how different communities celebrate festivals or address social issues. By emphasizing the value of diversity, an inclusive curriculum prepares students to live and work harmoniously in a pluralistic society.

The successful implementation of an inclusive curriculum relies heavily on the role of teachers. Educators must be equipped with the skills and knowledge necessary to adapt their teaching methods to the diverse needs of their students. This involves employing differentiated instruction, where lessons are customized to accommodate various learning styles, abilities, and cultural backgrounds. For example, a mathematics lesson might offer multiple problem-solving methods, allowing students to choose the approach that best suits their learning style. Teacher training programs, as recommended by the NEP 2020, should focus on enhancing educators' capacity to implement inclusive teaching practices that support a diverse student population.

6.4 Engaging with Multicultural Classrooms in Indian Cities

In India's swiftly urbanizing cities, classrooms are increasingly multicultural, with students hailing from diverse linguistic, cultural, and religious backgrounds. Effectively engaging with such heterogeneous classrooms necessitates that educators adopt culturally responsive and adaptable teaching methodologies. Multicultural classrooms present both opportunities and challenges: while students contribute unique perspectives and experiences, they may also encounter language barriers, cultural misunderstandings, and disparate socio-economic conditions. Culturally responsive teaching addresses these challenges by cultivating an inclusive, respectful, and dynamic learning environment in which all students feel valued and understood.

A fundamental strategy for engaging multicultural classrooms involves creating a learning environment that celebrates and respects diversity. Educators can implement activities and discussions that enable students to share their cultural backgrounds, traditions, and experiences. For instance, during festivals or national celebrations, students might present how these events are observed in their homes or communities, thereby providing insights into various traditions. This approach not only enriches the educational experience but also fosters mutual respect and understanding among students from diverse backgrounds. It encourages students to perceive cultural differences as opportunities for learning rather than impediments.

Language diversity is another salient feature of multicultural classrooms, particularly in urban settings where students often come from bilingual or multilingual households. Teachers must be attuned to these linguistic differences and provide support to students who may struggle with the language of instruction. For example, educators can utilize bilingual materials or permit students to articulate their thoughts in their native languages during discussions. Additionally, employing visual aids, gestures, and contextual explanations can aid students in comprehending complex concepts despite language barriers. The National Education Policy (NEP) 2020 advocates for the use of the mother tongue in early education, facilitating better understanding and engagement for students from diverse linguistic backgrounds.

Group work and peer collaboration are also effective strategies for enhancing engagement in multicultural classrooms. Collaborative projects allow students to learn from one another's perspectives and skills, fostering a more inclusive environment. By assigning diverse groups, teachers ensure that students from different cultural backgrounds work together, share ideas, and collectively solve problems. This interaction helps dismantle cultural barriers and promotes social cohesion, equipping students to function effectively in diverse teams in the future.

Another crucial strategy is the implementation of culturally relevant pedagogy, wherein educators incorporate examples, texts, and materials from the various cultural backgrounds of their students. In literature classes, for instance, teachers can include works by authors representing different linguistic and cultural communities within India. Similarly, in social studies, discussing historical events from multiple perspectives can help students appreciate the contributions of various communities to India's development. This approach ensures that students from all backgrounds see themselves reflected in the curriculum, thereby enhancing engagement and fostering a sense of belonging.

In urban areas, where students often originate from varying socio-economic backgrounds, teachers must be cognizant of the differing resources available to students at home. Some students may lack access to digital devices, private tutors, or extracurricular activities, which can lead to disparities in academic performance. To mitigate this, educators can design activities that do not heavily rely on external resources, ensuring that all students have the opportunity to participate fully, irrespective of their socio-economic status.

Establishing a safe and supportive classroom environment is also paramount for engaging multicultural classrooms. Educators must set clear norms for respectful communication and cultivate an atmosphere where students feel comfortable sharing their ideas and experiences. By actively discouraging discrimination, stereotyping, or exclusion, teachers ensure that the classroom remains a space where every student feels valued. Promoting open dialogue about cultural differences and similarities can help dispel misconceptions and foster a deeper understanding of diversity.

6.5 Overcoming Bias and Stereotypes in Indian Education

Biases and stereotypes within educational settings can significantly impair students' learning experiences, self-esteem, and overall academic achievement. In India, where classrooms exhibit extensive diversity in language, caste, religion, and socio-economic status, it is imperative to actively address these biases to cultivate an equitable and inclusive learning environment. Such prejudices may subtly permeate through textbook content, teacher expectations, or peer interactions. Mitigating these challenges necessitates deliberate efforts by educators to uphold fairness, equality, and respect.

A foundational step in overcoming classroom bias involves educators reflecting on their own assumptions and attitudes. Unconscious biases can shape how teachers interact with students, set expectations, and administer discipline or praise. For example, a teacher might inadvertently perceive students from certain socio-economic backgrounds as less capable or assume that girls are inherently less proficient in subjects like mathematics and science. These biases contribute to an unequal educational landscape. To counteract this, teachers should engage in regular self-reflection and pursue professional development opportunities focused on inclusivity and bias mitigation.

Curriculum design and textbook content play pivotal roles in either perpetuating or challenging stereotypes. Historically, Indian textbooks have often presented a limited perspective on history, culture, and society, frequently marginalizing contributions from groups such as Dalits, tribal communities, women, and religious minorities. Addressing these biases requires educators and policymakers to ensure that the curriculum accurately reflects the diversity of Indian society. This can be achieved by incorporating stories, case studies, and historical accounts from multiple perspectives, thereby ensuring fair representation of all communities. The National Education Policy (NEP) 2020 emphasizes the necessity of a more inclusive curriculum that highlights the contributions of all societal segments, fostering respect for diversity and social harmony.

Educators also have a crucial role in challenging stereotypes by promoting critical thinking and open discussion within the classroom. When biased statements emerge-whether originating from students, textbooks, or media-teachers should address them transparently and create opportunities for dialogue. For instance, if a student voices a stereotype regarding a particular caste, religion, or gender, the teacher can facilitate a discussion that explores the origins and detrimental impacts of such stereotypes. Encouraging students to question societal norms and biases aids in developing their empathy and fostering a more nuanced understanding of the world.

Fostering inclusive classroom practices is another effective strategy to mitigate bias. Teachers should ensure that all students, irrespective of their backgrounds, have equal opportunities to participate in activities and discussions. This might involve rotating group leadership roles to provide all students with the chance to lead or encouraging more reserved students to share their insights. By creating an environment where every voice is heard and respected, educators can dismantle societal hierarchies and stereotypes that often prevail outside the classroom.

Peer interactions present another avenue where biases and stereotypes can manifest, frequently through exclusion or bullying. In many Indian schools, students from marginalized communities or religious minorities may experience discrimination from their peers. Teachers must remain vigilant about these dynamics and promptly address incidents of bullying or exclusion. By fostering a culture of respect and empathy, educators can encourage students to value differences rather than perceive them as divisive. Organizing activities that promote teamwork and collaboration among students from diverse backgrounds can help eliminate barriers and build mutual respect.

Teacher expectations, influenced by stereotypes, can lead to self-fulfilling prophecies where students internalize low expectations based on their backgrounds and subsequently underperform. To counter this, teachers should maintain high, attainable expectations for all students and provide the necessary support to help them achieve these goals. Acknowledging and celebrating achievements across a diverse student body helps build confidence and cultivates a growth mindset, where students believe in their capacity to improve through effort and perseverance.

Promoting empathy and cross-cultural understanding stands out as one of the most effective means to overcome bias in education. Educators can create opportunities for students to learn about and from each other's cultural experiences. For example, organizing cultural exchange programs where students share their traditions, languages, and customs can help dismantle stereotypes and foster appreciation for diversity. Collaborative projects that require interaction across different cultural or socio-economic groups can deepen students' understanding of each other's perspectives and experiences.

6.6 Indigenous Knowledge and Local Culture in Teaching Methods

Integrating indigenous knowledge and local culture into pedagogical practices constitutes a fundamental aspect of culturally responsive education in India. Indigenous knowledge encompasses the traditional wisdom, practices, and skills transmitted across generations within communities, often pertaining to agriculture, health, environmental stewardship, and craftsmanship. Local culture comprises the customs, beliefs, languages, and traditions distinctive to specific regions. Incorporating these elements into the educational framework not only enriches students' learning experiences but also recognizes the significance of these cultural heritages within the contemporary education system.

India is home to a myriad of indigenous communities, each possessing its own rich traditions and knowledge systems. For centuries, these communities have developed sustainable practices intricately linked to their local environments. For instance, indigenous groups in the northeastern states have long employed sustainable agricultural methods such as shifting cultivation and water conservation, while tribal populations in central India hold extensive knowledge of medicinal plants and natural remedies. By embedding this knowledge into the curriculum, educators can provide students with practical insights into how traditional practices can address modern challenges like environmental conservation and sustainable development.

A primary advantage of integrating indigenous knowledge into education is the increased relevance of learning for students, particularly those from indigenous or rural backgrounds. Many Indian students originate from families where traditional practices remain integral to daily life. When these practices are mirrored in their education, students develop a stronger connection to the material they are studying. For example, in a science class, teachers might introduce traditional agricultural techniques utilized in students' communities, enabling them to relate theoretical concepts such as soil health and water conservation to practical, real-world applications. This approach not only enhances their comprehension but also fosters greater engagement with the subject matter.

Incorporating local culture into teaching methodologies also serves to promote cultural pride and identity among students. In numerous regions of India, students from indigenous or marginalized communities may perceive that their cultural heritage is undervalued or neglected within the mainstream education system. By integrating local traditions, narratives, and practices into the curriculum, educators can affirm the importance of these cultures and assist students in developing pride in their heritage. For instance, students in Gujarat might study the intricate art of Bandhani (tie-dye) as part of their lessons on traditional crafts, while students in Tamil Nadu could explore the cultural significance of Kolam (floor art) during festivals. These activities not only preserve cultural practices but also engage students in hands-on, experiential learning (Figure 6.2).

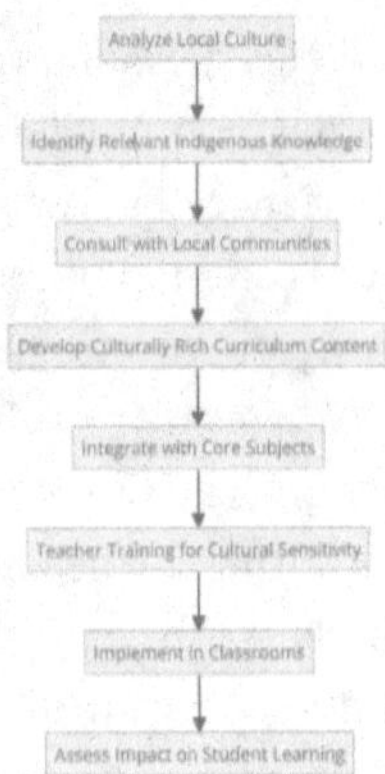

Figure 6.2: This flowchart shows how to **Incorporate Indigenous Knowledge** into the Indian school curriculum:

1. **Analyze Local Culture**: Understand local cultural elements.

2. **Identify Relevant Indigenous Knowledge**: Highlight key cultural knowledge that can be integrated.

3. **Consult with Local Communities**: Engage with community members to ensure cultural accuracy.

4. **Develop Culturally Rich Curriculum Content**: Create curriculum material that reflects local knowledge.

5. **Integrate with Core Subjects**: Blend indigenous knowledge into subjects like history, geography, and language.

6. **Teacher Training for Cultural Sensitivity**: Prepare teachers to handle cultural topics respectfully.

7. **Implement in Classrooms**: Apply the curriculum changes in school environments.

Assess Impact on Student Learning: Evaluate the effectiveness of the integration.

Incorporating indigenous knowledge and local culture into pedagogical practices is a critical element of culturally responsive education in India. Indigenous knowledge encompasses the traditional wisdom, practices, and skills that have been transmitted through generations within communities, often relating to agriculture, health, environmental stewardship, and craftsmanship. Local culture includes the customs, beliefs, languages, and traditions unique to specific regions. Integrating these elements into the classroom not only enriches students' learning experiences but also acknowledges the significance of these cultural heritages within the contemporary education system.

India hosts a diverse array of indigenous communities, each with its own rich traditions and knowledge systems. For centuries, these communities have developed sustainable practices intimately connected to their local environments. For instance, indigenous groups in the northeastern states have long employed sustainable agricultural methods such as shifting cultivation and water conservation, while tribal populations in central India possess extensive knowledge of medicinal plants and natural remedies. By embedding this knowledge into the curriculum, educators provide students with practical insights into how traditional practices can address modern challenges like environmental conservation and sustainable development.

A primary advantage of integrating indigenous knowledge into education is the increased relevance of learning for students, particularly those from indigenous or rural backgrounds. Many Indian students come from families where traditional practices remain integral to daily life. When these practices are reflected in their education, students develop a stronger connection to the material they are studying. For example, in a science class, teachers might introduce traditional agricultural techniques used in students' communities, enabling them to relate theoretical concepts such as soil health and water conservation to practical, real-world applications. This approach not only enhances comprehension but also fosters greater engagement with the subject matter.

Incorporating local culture into teaching methodologies also promotes cultural pride and identity among students. In numerous regions of India, students from indigenous or marginalized communities may perceive that their cultural heritage is undervalued or neglected within the mainstream education system. By integrating local traditions, narratives, and practices into the curriculum, educators affirm the importance of these cultures and assist students in developing pride in their heritage. For instance, students in Gujarat might study the intricate art of Bandhani (tie-dye) as part of their lessons on traditional crafts, while students in Tamil Nadu could explore the cultural significance of Kolam (floor art) during festivals. These activities not only preserve cultural practices but also engage students in hands-on, experiential learning (Figure 6.2).

Teachers can also integrate storytelling, a fundamental aspect of many indigenous traditions, into their instructional methods. Indigenous communities frequently transmit knowledge through oral traditions, including folktales, myths, and legends that convey moral lessons and practical wisdom. By embedding storytelling within lessons, educators can render complex concepts more accessible and engaging for students. For example, a teacher might employ a local folktale to introduce a lesson on environmental stewardship, illustrating how traditional narratives often emphasize the importance of living in harmony with nature. Storytelling also enhances listening skills, creativity, and critical thinking, as students are prompted to reflect on the lessons and themes inherent in these stories.

Field excursions and community engagement represent additional effective strategies for integrating indigenous knowledge and local culture into education. By taking students beyond the classroom to interact with local experts, artisans, or environmentalists, educators provide hands-on learning experiences directly connected to their cultural context. For instance, students might visit local farms to learn about organic farming techniques from traditional farmers or collaborate with local craftsmen to create pottery or textiles. These experiential learning opportunities enable students to connect academic content with their everyday lives and foster a deeper appreciation for the knowledge and skills prevalent within their communities.

The National Education Policy (NEP) 2020 supports the incorporation of local knowledge and culture into education, acknowledging that indigenous practices offer valuable insights into sustainability, resource management, and community living. The policy advocates for integrating traditional knowledge systems into the curriculum, particularly in areas such as environmental education, where indigenous practices provide sustainable solutions to contemporary challenges. By promoting these practices, the NEP aims to establish a more inclusive education system that recognizes the contributions of all cultural groups in India.

Educators also play a pivotal role in fostering respect for indigenous knowledge and local culture. They can encourage students to explore their own cultural heritage by assigning projects that involve interviewing elders, documenting traditional practices, or creating presentations on local history and customs. This not only aids students in learning more about their own culture but also promotes cross-cultural understanding among classmates from diverse backgrounds. By sharing their findings with the class, students can learn from each other's cultural experiences, fostering mutual respect and appreciation for diversity.

6.7 Role of Language Diversity in Indian Schools

India stands as one of the most linguistically diverse nations globally, boasting hundreds of languages across its various regions. This linguistic plurality offers both opportunities and challenges within the educational framework. In Indian schools, language is a critical determinant of students' learning experiences, particularly as many children originate from households where the spoken language differs from the medium of instruction. The National Education Policy (NEP) 2020 underscores the significance of mother tongue instruction in the early years of education, acknowledging that children assimilate knowledge more effectively when taught in a language with which they are most familiar. Embracing linguistic diversity within schools is essential for fostering an inclusive and efficacious learning environment that honors the linguistic identities of all students (Figure 6.3).

A primary rationale for valuing language diversity in Indian schools is its role in enhancing students' connection to their education. Numerous students, especially those in rural regions, experience a linguistic gap between their home environment and the language employed for schooling, leading to a sense of disjunction. Instruction in the mother tongue enables these students to better comprehend and engage with the educational material, resulting in improved academic outcomes. The NEP 2020 advocates for the provision of instruction in the mother tongue or local language during the foundational years, ensuring that students build a robust educational foundation before transitioning to other languages such as Hindi or English. This approach not only facilitates deeper understanding but also supports the preservation of linguistic heritage, thereby contributing to a more equitable and effective education system.

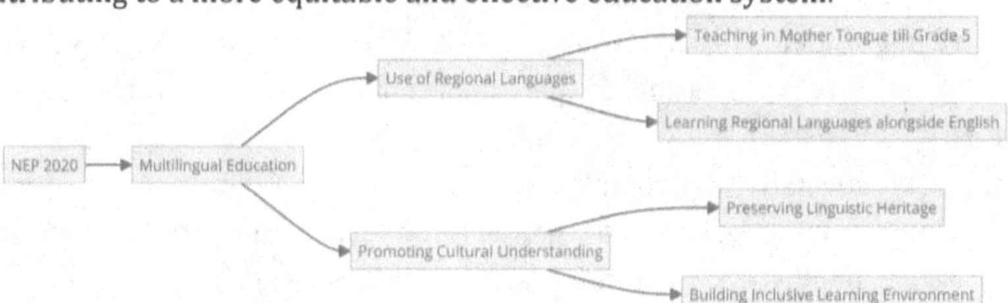

Figure 6.3: This diagram shows the role of **Language Diversity** in Indian schools as promoted by NEP 2020:

1. **Multilingual Education**: NEP 2020 promotes the use of multiple languages in education.

2. **Use of Regional Languages**: Schools are encouraged to use local languages as the medium of instruction.

o **Teaching in Mother Tongue**: Emphasis on using the mother tongue till Grade 5.

o **Learning Regional Languages Alongside English**: Students are exposed to both local languages and English.

3. **Promoting Cultural Understanding**: Language diversity helps in preserving cultural and linguistic heritage and creates an inclusive learning environment.

In classrooms where students communicate in diverse languages, it is imperative for educators to employ multilingual strategies to accommodate all learners effectively. For instance, educators can integrate bilingual materials, utilize visual aids, and facilitate peer teaching, wherein students proficient in the language of instruction assist those still acquiring it. Furthermore, permitting students to articulate their thoughts in their native languages during discussions or assignments can bridge the gap between their linguistic identities and academic pursuits. These approaches foster a more inclusive classroom environment, positioning language as a tool for enhanced comprehension rather than a hindrance to participation.

Another critical facet of embracing linguistic diversity in Indian educational institutions is the cultivation of respect for all languages. In numerous educational contexts, English is often perceived as the dominant language, while regional languages or dialects may be undervalued. This linguistic hierarchy can engender feelings of inferiority among students who speak regional languages at home, adversely impacting their self-esteem and confidence. To mitigate this, schools should advocate for the recognition that all languages hold equal value and that multilingualism constitutes an asset. One effective method is encouraging students to share stories, songs, or cultural practices in their native languages, thereby fostering a classroom milieu that celebrates linguistic diversity.

Language diversity also significantly contributes to the promotion of cross-cultural understanding. In India's multicultural classrooms, students originate from varied linguistic and cultural backgrounds, with language serving as a fundamental aspect of their identities. By encouraging students to explore and respect each other's languages, educators can cultivate empathy and mutual respect. For example, implementing a "language of the week" activity, where students take turns teaching basic phrases in their native languages to their peers, can stimulate interest in different languages and enhance appreciation for the linguistic diversity present within the classroom.

The National Education Policy (NEP) 2020 underscores the importance of multilingual education for cognitive development and future opportunities. The policy endorses the "three-language formula," which advocates for students to learn three languages: their mother tongue, a regional language, and a foreign language such as English. This strategy aims to promote multilingualism, ensuring that students acquire the language competencies necessary to thrive in a globalized environment while maintaining a strong connection to their cultural and linguistic heritage.

Beyond cognitive and cultural advantages, multilingual education enhances students' problem-solving and critical thinking skills. Research indicates that learning multiple languages enhances cognitive flexibility, as students continuously navigate different linguistic systems. This mental adaptability can translate into improved academic performance across various disciplines, as students develop the capacity to approach problems from multiple perspectives. In the context of Indian schools, where linguistic diversity is inherent to the educational landscape, fostering multilingualism provides students with a cognitive edge that extends beyond mere language acquisition.

6.8 Incorporating Regional and Traditional Knowledge into Curriculum

Incorporating regional and traditional knowledge into the curriculum constitutes a pivotal initiative in establishing an inclusive and culturally responsive education system in India. Given the nation's vast cultural diversity and extensive heritage of traditional wisdom, India possesses a significant repository of knowledge that has been transmitted through generations. This includes expertise in domains such as agriculture, medicine, art, architecture, and environmental sustainability, all deeply embedded in local practices. By integrating these elements into the educational framework, schools can render education more pertinent to students' lives while simultaneously preserving and honoring India's cultural legacy. The National Education Policy (NEP) 2020 underscores the importance of embedding local knowledge systems within the curriculum to afford students a more comprehensive understanding of the world.

A primary advantage of embedding regional and traditional knowledge into education lies in its ability to connect learning with students' immediate environments. For pupils in rural areas, where traditional practices like farming, weaving, or herbal medicine remain essential, incorporating these subjects into the curriculum bridges the gap between home and school. For instance, in agricultural regions, students might study soil health, irrigation techniques, and sustainable farming practices by examining local methods that have been refined over generations. This approach not only enhances students' grasp of academic disciplines such as science and environmental studies but also instills a sense of pride in their cultural heritage.

The integration of traditional knowledge is equally critical for promoting sustainability and environmental stewardship. Indigenous and regional communities in India have long adhered to sustainable living practices, ranging from water conservation techniques in arid regions to forest management strategies in mountainous areas. By teaching these methods within the classroom, educators can impart valuable lessons in environmental conservation rooted in local traditions. For example, students in Rajasthan might explore traditional water conservation techniques like stepwells (baolis) and rainwater harvesting systems that have enabled communities to thrive in dry climates. This not only deepens students' understanding of environmental science but also provides practical solutions to contemporary environmental challenges.

Art, music, and crafts represent additional areas where regional knowledge can be seamlessly integrated into the curriculum. India's traditional arts, such as Madhubani painting from Bihar, Kathak dance from Uttar Pradesh, or Carnatic music from Tamil Nadu, are replete with historical significance, cultural richness, and artistic techniques. Incorporating these art forms into the curriculum enables schools to foster an appreciation for India's artistic heritage while teaching students creative expression and craftsmanship. Schools can invite local artisans or performers to demonstrate traditional arts, thereby facilitating hands-on learning experiences that extend beyond conventional textbook instruction. This not only nurtures creativity but also aids in the preservation of these cultural practices for future generations (Figure 6.2).

Another effective method for integrating regional and traditional knowledge is through storytelling and oral traditions, which are deeply ingrained in many of India's communities. Folktales, myths, and legends often encapsulate moral lessons, historical insights, and cultural values passed down orally. Educators can utilize these narratives as pedagogical tools for teaching language, ethics, and history, thereby helping students connect with their cultural roots while developing critical thinking and analytical skills. For example, a teacher might employ a local folktale to illustrate the importance of environmental conservation or community values, prompting students to reflect on how these stories relate to contemporary issues.

Incorporating traditional knowledge into the curriculum also supports the development of vocational skills, particularly in rural areas where such skills are integral to livelihoods. Schools in regions renowned for traditional crafts like pottery, textile weaving, or carpentry can offer courses that teach these skills alongside academic subjects. This provides students with valuable vocational training while safeguarding traditional craftsmanship that might otherwise be lost. For instance, in Kutch, Gujarat, students could learn the intricate art of embroidery, while those in Odisha might study the ancient craft of stone carving. These courses equip students with skills that can lead to economic opportunities within their communities.

The NEP 2020 advocates for the inclusion of regional and traditional knowledge in education, recognizing that these knowledge systems offer critical insights into sustainable living, resource management, and community building. The policy promotes the integration of local knowledge across all educational levels, particularly within subjects such as environmental science, social studies, and vocational training. By endorsing traditional knowledge, the NEP aims to cultivate a more inclusive and contextually relevant education system that values India's diverse cultural heritage.

Educators play an essential role in embedding regional and traditional knowledge into the curriculum. They can design lessons that reflect local traditions and engage students in experiential learning activities that connect classroom concepts with real-world practices. For example, teachers might organize field trips to local farms, workshops, or cultural sites where students can observe traditional practices firsthand. In history classes, educators could invite local elders to share their knowledge about historical events or cultural practices, thereby providing students with firsthand accounts that enrich their understanding of the past. Through these initiatives, teachers help bridge the gap between academic learning and cultural heritage, fostering a more holistic and engaging educational experience for all students.

CHAPTER 7

MINDFULNESS AND EMOTIONAL EARNING

7.1 The Connection Between Mindfulness and Learning in Indian Schools

Mindfulness, characterized by full presence and awareness of the current moment, has garnered increasing attention in educational settings due to its beneficial impacts on student learning and well-being. Within Indian schools, where students frequently encounter academic pressures, societal expectations, and intense competition, mindfulness serves as a valuable tool for enhancing concentration, mitigating stress, and fostering emotional resilience. By facilitating the development of greater self-awareness and emotional regulation, mindfulness can augment the overall learning experience and support mental health.

The relationship between mindfulness and learning is predicated on the notion that when students are fully present, they can concentrate more effectively, process information more thoroughly, and engage more deeply with their lessons. In a typical Indian classroom, where the volume of material can be overwhelming, mindfulness practices can help students decelerate and concentrate on the immediate task. This approach encourages sustained attention during lessons, minimizes distractions, and enables students to approach challenges with a calm and clear mindset. Consequently, mindfulness can bolster academic performance by cultivating a more focused and engaged learning environment.

Moreover, mindfulness holds particular significance in Indian schools, where students often endure elevated stress levels due to the emphasis on examinations, grades, and career prospects. The competitive nature of the education system can result in anxiety and burnout, especially among older students preparing for board examinations or entrance assessments for higher education. Mindfulness equips students with strategies to manage these pressures by teaching techniques such as deep breathing and maintaining present-moment awareness during stressful situations. This fosters emotional resilience, enabling students to cope with academic demands more effectively and reducing the likelihood of burnout.

Beyond enhancing academic focus and emotional resilience, mindfulness also improves students' social and emotional competencies. By promoting self-reflection and empathy, mindfulness aids students in gaining a deeper understanding of their own emotions and those of others. This is particularly important in multicultural Indian classrooms, where students from diverse backgrounds may require support in navigating social interactions. Mindfulness nurtures kindness, empathy, and cooperation, thereby cultivating a more positive and inclusive classroom environment where students feel safe and respected.

The National Education Policy (NEP) 2020 acknowledges the critical role of mental health and emotional well-being in education, advocating for the integration of life skills such as emotional regulation, stress management, and empathy into the curriculum. Mindfulness aligns with these objectives by providing students with practical tools to manage their emotions and remain grounded in challenging situations. By embedding mindfulness practices into daily school routines, Indian schools can establish a more supportive learning environment that prioritizes the holistic development of students.

Several Indian schools have already successfully incorporated mindfulness practices, often through brief breathing exercises or guided meditation sessions at the beginning of the school day. These exercises assist students in centering themselves, alleviating tension, and establishing a positive tone for the day ahead. Additionally, teachers can introduce mindfulness moments during transitions between lessons, allowing students to pause, refocus, and re-engage with subsequent tasks. These small, consistent mindfulness practices can significantly enhance students' ability to maintain focus and manage their emotions throughout the school day (Figure 7.1).

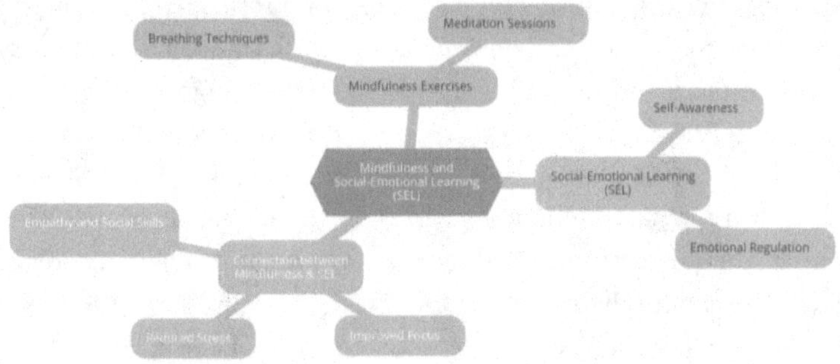

Figure 7.1: This mind map illustrates the connection between **Mindfulness Exercises** and **Social-Emotional Learning (SEL)** in Indian schools:

1. **Mindfulness Exercises**:

o Techniques like breathing exercises and meditation help students focus and manage stress.

2. **Social-Emotional Learning (SEL)**:
o Focuses on self-awareness and emotional regulation to help students better understand and manage their emotions.

3. **Connection between Mindfulness & SEL**:
o Combining mindfulness with SEL improves focus, reduces stress, and enhances empathy and social skills.

Mindfulness is also closely tied to improving self-regulation, a key factor in academic success. When students learn how to manage their emotions and impulses, they are better able to handle distractions, persist through difficult tasks, and maintain motivation. In the Indian context, where students often experience intense academic pressures, the ability to self-regulate is essential for maintaining a balanced approach to their studies. Mindfulness teaches students to observe their thoughts and feelings without judgment, helping them stay calm and focused, even when faced with challenges.

7.2 Implementing Social-Emotional Learning (SEL) in Indian Classrooms

Social-Emotional Learning (SEL) concentrates on cultivating essential life skills in students, including emotional regulation, empathy, relationship-building, and responsible decision-making. Within Indian classrooms, where academic pressures and a highly competitive environment are prevalent, the implementation of SEL can markedly enhance emotional well-being and improve students' capacity to manage stress. SEL contributes to a positive school culture by fostering self-awareness, emotional intelligence, and social competencies, thereby creating more supportive and inclusive learning environments.

A principal advantage of SEL lies in its focus on emotional regulation, enabling students to manage their emotions healthily. In the Indian education system, where the emphasis on examinations, societal expectations, and peer pressure can be intense, students frequently grapple with anxiety and frustration. SEL equips students with the ability to identify and comprehend their emotions, providing them with techniques such as deep breathing, mindfulness, and cognitive reframing to handle these feelings. By mastering emotional regulation, students can enhance their concentration in class, reduce disruptive behaviors, and build resilience against challenges.

SEL also emphasizes the development of empathy and relationship-building, which are particularly significant in India's diverse and multicultural schools. With students originating from a multitude of cultural, religious, and socio-economic backgrounds, fostering empathy is essential for creating an inclusive and respectful school environment. Through SEL activities, students learn to appreciate different perspectives, engage in active listening, and communicate more effectively with their peers. This not only mitigates instances of bullying or exclusion but also strengthens classroom cohesion and promotes collaborative learning.

The integration of SEL into Indian classrooms necessitates a structured approach that embeds social-emotional learning within the existing curriculum. This can be accomplished through direct instruction, where educators allocate time to specific SEL lessons addressing topics such as self-awareness, emotional regulation, and interpersonal skills. For example, teachers might incorporate activities that prompt students to reflect on their emotions, engage in role-playing social scenarios, or practice conflict-resolution strategies. These lessons can be seamlessly integrated into subjects like language arts or social studies, allowing students to explore the emotional and social dimensions of literature or historical events.

Experiential learning activities further enhance the implementation of SEL by enabling students to apply these skills in real-life contexts. Group projects and cooperative learning tasks offer opportunities for students to practice teamwork, communication, and problem-solving in collaborative settings. Additionally, peer mediation initiatives, where students assist in resolving conflicts among classmates, foster a sense of responsibility and empathy. These activities facilitate the internalization of SEL principles, equipping students with the confidence to navigate social interactions both within and beyond the classroom.

SEL also plays a pivotal role in promoting responsible decision-making. In the fast-paced academic environment of Indian schools, students often face pressure to make swift decisions regarding their studies, social relationships, and future careers. SEL aids students in developing critical thinking skills, enabling them to evaluate options, consider the consequences of their actions, and make informed choices. For instance, students trained in SEL are more likely to pause and reflect on their emotions before responding impulsively in stressful situations. This ability to make deliberate decisions contributes to their overall well-being and academic success.

Educators are central to the effective implementation of SEL in Indian classrooms. They must not only instruct these skills but also exemplify them in their interactions with students. Teachers who demonstrate empathy, active listening, and emotional regulation provide positive models for students to emulate. Furthermore, teacher training programs are essential in equipping educators with the necessary tools and strategies to integrate SEL into their teaching practices effectively. The National Education Policy (NEP) 2020 recognizes the importance of teacher training in social-emotional competencies, highlighting the need for educators to support the emotional and social development of students.

Parental involvement is another critical factor in the success of SEL initiatives. Schools can engage parents by providing resources and workshops on reinforcing social-emotional learning at home. This collaboration ensures that students receive consistent messages about emotional intelligence, empathy, and responsible decision-making both in school and within their families. When parents and teachers work together, students are more likely to develop robust social-emotional skills that benefit them throughout their academic journeys and beyond.

7.3 Mindfulness Exercises for Students in India

Mindfulness exercises have demonstrated efficacy in assisting students to manage stress, enhance focus, and promote emotional well-being. Within the context of Indian schools, where students frequently encounter pressures from academic demands, societal expectations, and extracurricular activities, mindfulness serves as a straightforward yet potent mechanism for achieving balance and emotional stability. The integration of mindfulness exercises into daily routines can significantly influence students' ability to concentrate on their studies, regulate emotions, and maintain a sense of tranquility throughout the day.

Among the most accessible mindfulness practices for students is focused breathing. This technique involves directing attention to the breath, meticulously observing each inhale and exhale without judgment. Focused breathing contributes to the relaxation of both the mind and body, thereby facilitating improved concentration and the management of stress or anxiety. Educators can conduct simple focused breathing sessions at the commencement of the school day or prior to examinations, guiding students to sit quietly, close their eyes, and engage in slow, deep breaths. Even brief periods of this practice can enable students to feel more grounded and prepared to engage actively in their lessons.

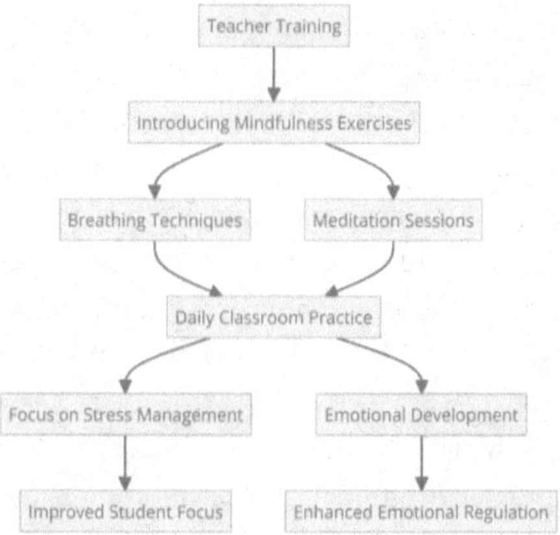

Figure 7.2: This diagram outlines the steps for **Implementing Mindfulness in Classrooms**:

1. **Teacher Training**: Prepare teachers to guide mindfulness exercises.

2. **Introducing Mindfulness Exercises**: Incorporate practices like breathing techniques and meditation sessions.

3. **Daily Classroom Practice**: Regular implementation in daily routines.

4. **Focus on Stress Management and Emotional Development**: Use mindfulness to help students manage stress and develop emotional regulation.

5. **Outcomes**: Improved student focus and emotional control.

Mindfulness exercises have emerged as effective strategies for aiding students in managing stress, enhancing focus, and promoting emotional well-being. In the context of Indian schools, where students frequently contend with academic pressures, societal expectations, and numerous extracurricular commitments, mindfulness provides a straightforward yet potent mechanism for achieving emotional balance and stability. The incorporation of mindfulness exercises into daily routines can positively influence students' capacity to concentrate on their studies, regulate emotions, and sustain a sense of calm throughout the day.

One of the most accessible mindfulness practices for students is focused breathing. This technique involves guiding students to concentrate on their breath, attentively observing each inhale and exhale without judgment. Focused breathing serves to calm both the mind and body, thereby facilitating improved concentration and the management of stress or anxiety. Educators can implement simple focused breathing sessions at the beginning of the school day or preceding examinations, encouraging students to sit quietly, close their eyes, and engage in slow, deep breaths. Even brief periods of this practice can help students feel more grounded and prepared to participate actively in their lessons.

Another effective mindfulness exercise is the body scan, where students are guided to direct their awareness to different parts of their body, noting any tension or discomfort and releasing it with each breath. The body scan enhances students' attunement to their physical sensations, thereby improving their overall sense of well-being and relaxation. For instance, after prolonged periods of sitting in class, teachers can lead a short body scan to help students stretch and alleviate any bodily tension, which in turn enhances their focus and readiness to learn (Figure 7.2).

Mindful listening is another exercise that encourages students to concentrate on sounds within their environment. In the often bustling environment of an Indian classroom, mindful listening aids students in minimizing distractions and improving their focus. Educators can initiate the exercise by instructing students to sit quietly and listen to the ambient sounds, such as birds outside, footsteps in the hallway, or the hum of a fan. After a minute or two, students can share what they heard, thereby fostering a heightened awareness of their surroundings and enhancing their concentration skills.

Visualization stands out as a powerful mindfulness exercise that assists students in managing stress and boosting creativity. In this practice, students are guided to envision a peaceful place or a positive outcome, such as a serene beach, a forest, or successfully completing a challenging task. Visualization helps students divert their focus from negative or stressful thoughts to calming or motivating images. For example, prior to a stressful exam, teachers can guide students through a visualization exercise where they imagine themselves feeling calm, confident, and capable of performing optimally. This technique aids in reducing anxiety and enhancing performance.

Gratitude practices constitute another mindfulness tool that benefits students emotionally. By dedicating time each day to reflect on things they are grateful for, students can cultivate a more positive mindset and bolster their emotional resilience. Educators can incorporate this into the classroom by commencing each day with a "gratitude circle," where students share one aspect they are thankful for. This simple exercise encourages students to focus on positive elements of their lives and fosters a sense of community within the classroom.

Mindfulness journaling offers another avenue for students to reflect on their thoughts and emotions in a structured manner. Educators can provide prompts such as "What are you feeling right now?" or "What made you feel calm today?" This exercise encourages self-reflection and the development of greater emotional awareness. Journaling also offers students an outlet for processing their feelings, which can be particularly beneficial for those who find verbal expression challenging.

Mindful walking is an activity particularly beneficial for students who may feel restless or distracted after extended periods of sitting. In mindful walking, students focus on the sensations of each step-their feet contacting the ground, the movement of their legs, and the rhythm of their breath. This exercise helps students reconnect with their bodies and provides a calming break from academic tasks. Educators can integrate mindful walking into outdoor activities or transitions between classes to help students reset and refocus.

The advantages of mindfulness exercises for students are supported by research indicating that such practices can reduce stress, improve attention, and enhance emotional regulation. In Indian schools, where academic pressure is often intense, these exercises offer practical tools for students to manage stress and enhance focus. By embedding mindfulness exercises into the school day, educators can foster a more balanced and emotionally supportive learning environment.

7.4 Creating a Positive Learning Environment in Indian Schools

A positive learning environment is fundamental to fostering student engagement, academic achievement, and emotional well-being. In Indian schools, where students frequently navigate high levels of stress due to academic pressures, cultivating classrooms that are nurturing, inclusive, and supportive is paramount. Such environments enable students to feel safe, valued, and motivated to learn, thereby fostering a sense of belonging that enhances both their academic and personal development.

Central to a positive learning environment is the establishment of strong relationships between teachers and students. In the context of Indian classrooms, where the teacher is often perceived as an authority figure, creating an atmosphere of mutual respect and trust is essential. Educators who invest time in understanding their students' individual needs and demonstrate genuine concern for their well-being can cultivate a more open and collaborative learning space. When students perceive that their teachers respect and care for them, they are more inclined to engage actively in the learning process and participate fully in classroom activities.

Promoting inclusivity and celebrating diversity are also critical components of a positive learning environment. India's multicultural society encompasses a wide range of cultural, linguistic, and socio-economic backgrounds. A positive learning environment acknowledges and embraces this diversity by ensuring that every student feels represented and respected, irrespective of their background. Educators can achieve this by incorporating culturally relevant examples into lessons, encouraging students to share their experiences, and facilitating open discussions about diversity. This approach not only strengthens students' connections to their education but also fosters empathy and respect among classmates.

Encouraging collaboration and teamwork serves as another effective strategy for creating a positive learning environment. In Indian classrooms, where individual performance and competition are often emphasized, promoting group work and peer learning helps build a sense of community and support. Collaborative projects and assignments enable students to develop essential social skills such as communication, cooperation, and problem-solving. These activities provide opportunities for students to learn from one another, share ideas, and form stronger relationships with their peers, thereby enhancing both academic learning and the overall classroom culture.

Emphasizing emotional safety is equally important in fostering a positive learning environment. Students must feel comfortable expressing their thoughts, asking questions, and making mistakes without fear of judgment or ridicule. In many traditional Indian classrooms, there is a prevalent fear of failure or embarrassment if students do not provide the correct answer. Educators can counteract this by creating a supportive atmosphere where mistakes are viewed as integral to the learning process, encouraging students to take risks and explore new ideas. For example, teachers can commend students for their effort and creativity rather than solely for correct responses, reinforcing the notion that learning is a journey of growth and improvement.

Establishing clear classroom routines and expectations further contributes to a positive learning environment. In Indian schools, where classroom sizes can be large, it is essential for educators to set explicit rules and routines that promote respect, cooperation, and responsibility. When students understand what is expected of them and know how to behave in various situations, they are more likely to feel secure and focused in their learning. Involving students in the development of classroom norms can encourage them to take ownership of their behavior and contribute to a positive classroom culture.

The physical environment of the classroom also plays a significant role in creating a positive learning space. Although many Indian schools may face limitations in terms of infrastructure or resources, thoughtful arrangements can make a substantial difference. Classrooms that are clean, organized, and equipped with stimulating materials can enhance the learning experience and increase student engagement. Displaying student work, incorporating vibrant colors, or setting up learning stations can make the classroom more inviting and foster a sense of pride in the learning process. Even in resource-constrained settings, teachers can create a welcoming and positive atmosphere through the strategic arrangement of space and the utilization of available materials.

Celebrating student achievements, both large and small, is a powerful method for boosting motivation and establishing a positive classroom environment. Recognizing students for their hard work, improvement, and contributions fosters a sense of accomplishment and encourages continued striving for success. Educators can employ positive reinforcement techniques, such as praise, certificates, or classroom awards, to acknowledge students' efforts. By celebrating achievements, teachers not only enhance students' self-esteem but also contribute to a more encouraging and supportive classroom culture.

The significance of emotional well-being is central to creating a positive learning environment, as highlighted by the National Education Policy (NEP) 2020, which advocates for a focus on holistic development. Incorporating mindfulness practices, Social-Emotional Learning (SEL), and stress management strategies are vital components of a learning environment that addresses students' emotional needs. Integrating mindfulness exercises, facilitating open discussions about emotions, and teaching students coping strategies for stress contribute to a classroom atmosphere that is not only academically oriented but also emotionally supportive.

7.5 Measuring the Impact of Emotional Learning in Indian Context

Assessing the impact of Social-Emotional Learning (SEL) in Indian educational institutions is vital for determining the efficacy with which students develop the essential social and emotional competencies necessary for their comprehensive growth. SEL encompasses skills such as emotional regulation, empathy, resilience, and interpersonal communication. While academic performance is typically gauged through examinations and standardized assessments, evaluating the effects of SEL necessitates distinct methodologies that focus on students' emotional well-being, relationships, and behavioral patterns.

In India, where academic success is frequently prioritized, the incorporation of emotional learning into the curriculum remains a relatively nascent endeavor. The National Education Policy (NEP) 2020 underscores the significance of holistic education, recognizing that emotional learning is as crucial as academic achievement. By fostering SEL skills, students are better prepared to manage stress, cultivate positive relationships, and make informed decisions. To effectively measure the impact of emotional learning, educational institutions must employ tools and strategies that assess both qualitative and quantitative dimensions of students' emotional development.

One effective method for measuring emotional learning is through self-assessment. Encouraging students to reflect on their emotions, relationships, and behaviors fosters greater self-awareness. For example, educators can utilize SEL surveys or journals where students evaluate their emotional responses in various scenarios, their stress management capabilities, or their interactions with peers. These self-assessments not only heighten students' consciousness of their emotional states but also enable educators to evaluate the extent to which students are applying SEL strategies in their daily lives.

Teacher observations constitute another critical component in measuring SEL. Educators are often the first to detect changes in student behavior, attitudes, and interpersonal relationships. By observing students during classroom discussions, group activities, or conflict situations, teachers can assess the application of emotional regulation techniques, demonstrations of empathy, and levels of cooperation. Documenting these observations allows for the identification of behavioral improvements or areas requiring additional support, providing valuable insights into students' social-emotional development over time.

Peer assessments offer an additional avenue for evaluating SEL. By soliciting feedback from students regarding their classmates' behaviors and interactions during collaborative projects or group tasks, educators can gain diverse perspectives on the social dynamics within the classroom. For instance, peers might assess how effectively their classmates listen, contribute to discussions, or resolve conflicts. This method not only encourages students to reflect on their own and others' social skills but also promotes accountability and mutual respect. Moreover, peer assessments provide teachers with supplementary data on how SEL is manifested in real-world interactions.

Structured SEL assessments, specifically designed to measure social-emotional competencies, are also instrumental in evaluating the impact of emotional learning. These assessments typically involve questionnaires or rating scales that evaluate key aspects of SEL, such as emotional regulation, empathy, and relationship-building. For example, an SEL assessment might inquire how frequently students can remain calm under pressure or how often they assist their peers in need. Such assessments furnish schools with quantifiable data on students' social-emotional progress, facilitating the identification of trends and areas necessitating further intervention.

Attendance and disciplinary records serve as indirect indicators of the effectiveness of SEL programs. Schools implementing SEL initiatives often observe improved attendance rates, a reduction in behavioral issues, and enhanced relationships between students and teachers. Monitoring changes in attendance and discipline over time can provide insights into the broader impacts of SEL on student engagement and conduct. For instance, a decline in classroom disruptions or bullying incidents may signify that students are developing stronger emotional regulation and empathy skills.

Parental feedback is another essential component in assessing SEL within Indian schools. Parents can offer valuable perspectives on how well students are applying SEL skills outside the classroom, such as at home or in social settings. Schools can collect this feedback through surveys or parent-teacher meetings, wherein parents share observations about their child's emotional well-being, behavior, and relationships. For example, parents might report improvements in their child's ability to manage stress during exams or resolve conflicts with siblings. This external feedback complements school-based assessments, providing a more comprehensive understanding of the impact of SEL on students' lives.

Long-term outcome tracking is crucial for evaluating the sustained effects of SEL. Students who develop robust SEL skills are more likely to achieve success in future academic and professional endeavors, as these skills are closely linked to resilience, effective communication, and problem-solving abilities. Educational institutions can monitor students' progress as they advance through different grade levels, examining correlations between SEL development and academic performance, leadership qualities, or participation in extracurricular activities. Adopting a longitudinal approach allows schools to assess how emotional learning contributes to students' enduring success and well-being.

The NEP 2020 highlights the imperative of holistic education, which encompasses emotional well-being alongside academic development. Measuring the impact of SEL is integral to this vision, enabling schools to ensure that they are not only achieving academic objectives but also fostering the social and emotional growth of their students. As SEL programs become more prevalent in Indian schools, refining assessment methodologies to accurately capture the breadth of students' emotional development will be essential. Through comprehensive evaluation strategies, Indian educational institutions can better support the holistic development of their students, aligning with the NEP 2020's emphasis on creating well-rounded, emotionally resilient individuals.

7.6 Role of Teachers and Parents in Emotional Development

Teachers and parents are instrumental in the emotional development of children, particularly within Indian schools where students frequently encounter significant academic and social pressures. Emotional development is a critical component of a child's overall growth, encompassing the ability to recognize, express, and manage emotions, establish healthy relationships, and cultivate empathy and resilience. Both educators and parents serve as essential role models and guides in this process, aiding children in navigating the complexities of their emotional experiences.

Educators, as primary figures in students' daily academic lives, exert a direct influence on how children understand and manage their emotions. In Indian educational contexts, where academic achievement is often emphasized, teachers are uniquely positioned to integrate emotional development into the learning environment. By fostering a classroom culture that values emotional intelligence, teachers can create a safe space where students feel comfortable expressing their feelings and discussing their emotional challenges. For instance, teachers can facilitate class discussions on managing exam-related stress, encourage students to share their thoughts in group settings, and promote kindness and respect among peers.

A key mechanism through which teachers contribute to emotional development is by modeling emotionally intelligent behavior. When educators demonstrate empathy, active listening, and emotional regulation, students learn by observing these behaviors. For example, a teacher who calmly resolves a classroom conflict or responds to a stressful situation with patience and composure provides a tangible example for students to emulate. This form of role modeling is especially significant in Indian classrooms, where students often view teachers as authority figures and guides for appropriate behavior in both academic and social contexts.

Additionally, teachers play a crucial role in teaching students social-emotional skills, which are essential for emotional maturation. By incorporating Social-Emotional Learning (SEL) into their daily lessons, educators can help students build self-awareness, empathy, and relationship-building skills. For example, teachers might introduce activities that encourage students to reflect on their emotions, set personal goals, or resolve interpersonal conflicts constructively.

These activities equip students with the tools needed to manage their emotional lives both inside and outside the classroom. The National Education Policy (NEP) 2020 emphasizes the importance of integrating SEL into the curriculum to support students' holistic development, thereby highlighting the pivotal role of teachers in this process (Figure 7.3).

Beyond teaching and modeling emotional intelligence, teachers can cultivate an emotionally supportive classroom environment that encourages positive interactions and mutual respect. By fostering a sense of community, educators help students feel connected to their peers and more secure within the school environment. This can be achieved through group activities, peer collaboration, and open discussions about emotions and social dynamics. When students feel supported by both their teachers and classmates, they are more likely to develop a positive self-image and adopt healthy emotional habits.

In summary, the roles of teachers and parents are indispensable in the emotional development of children within Indian schools. By modeling emotionally intelligent behavior, integrating SEL into the curriculum, and creating supportive and inclusive classroom environments, educators can significantly enhance students' emotional well-being and overall growth. These efforts align with the NEP 2020's emphasis on holistic education, ensuring that students not only achieve academic success but also develop the emotional and social competencies necessary for their comprehensive development.

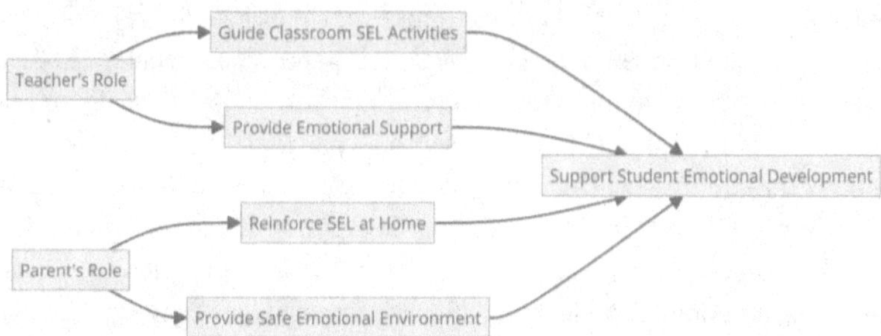

Figure 7.3: This flowchart outlines the **Roles of Teachers and Parents** in supporting students' emotional and social development:

1. **Teacher's Role:**
   o Guide classroom SEL (Social-Emotional Learning) activities.
   o Provide emotional support to students.
2. **Parent's Role:**
   o Reinforce SEL practices at home.

o Provide a safe emotional environment.

3. **Outcome**: Together, teachers and parents support students' emotional development.

Parents hold a pivotal role in a child's emotional development beyond the educational setting. The emotional support and guidance provided at home profoundly influence children's understanding and regulation of their emotions. In the context of Indian families, where cultural and societal norms often prioritize academic achievement, parents can mitigate these pressures by fostering their children's emotional well-being. By promoting open dialogue, attentively addressing their children's concerns, and affirming their emotions, parents establish a household environment conducive to emotional maturation.

A fundamental way parents enhance their child's emotional development is by creating a secure environment for emotional expression. In numerous Indian households, conversations about emotions frequently take a backseat to discussions centered on academics or pragmatic issues. Nonetheless, when parents intentionally engage in conversations about feelings-be it academic stress, interpersonal frustrations, or joy over accomplishments-they equip their children with the vocabulary and confidence necessary to articulate their emotions. Such transparent communication ensures that children feel acknowledged and supported, which is essential for cultivating emotional resilience.

Additionally, parents play a significant role in emotional development by imparting coping mechanisms for handling stress and challenging emotions. For instance, parents can exemplify effective stress management techniques, such as relaxation practices, mindfulness activities, or calmly addressing problems instead of reacting impulsively. Observing these behaviors increases the likelihood that children will adopt similar strategies in their own lives. Within the Indian framework, where students often face pressure from both educational institutions and familial expectations, these coping strategies are vital for maintaining emotional equilibrium and managing stress effectively.

The collaboration between educators and parents is crucial in fostering the emotional development of students. When both entities collaborate, they can offer consistent guidance and reinforcement of emotional learning both in educational and home environments. Regular interactions between teachers and parents regarding a child's emotional progress can facilitate the early identification of challenges and ensure a unified approach between school and family. For example, if a teacher notices a student grappling with anxiety or social relationships, they can liaise with the parents to formulate supportive strategies at home. Conversely, parents can provide insights into their child's emotional experiences outside school, enabling teachers to tailor their support within the classroom effectively.

Educational institutions can support this collaboration by organizing parent-teacher conferences, workshops, and informational sessions focused on emotional development and social-emotional learning (SEL) strategies. These initiatives can equip parents with the necessary tools and techniques to nurture their child's emotional health and create a platform for addressing the emotional challenges faced by students in today's competitive and fast-paced environment. The National Education Policy (NEP) 2020 advocates for strengthened partnerships between schools and families to promote a holistic approach to education, encompassing emotional development.

7.7 Mindfulness and Stress Management Techniques for Indian Students

Mindfulness and stress management strategies are gaining prominence within the Indian educational landscape, where students frequently encounter substantial academic pressures. The highly competitive examination environment, coupled with societal expectations and the pursuit of excellence, contributes to elevated levels of stress, anxiety, and burnout among learners. In response to these issues, educational institutions are increasingly integrating mindfulness practices and stress mitigation techniques aimed at fostering mental and emotional equilibrium. These approaches not only alleviate stress but also enhance concentration, emotional regulation, and overall well-being, aligning with the holistic educational objectives outlined in the National Education Policy (NEP) 2020.

Mindfulness interventions are particularly beneficial for students as they cultivate present-moment awareness, thereby enhancing focus and diminishing anxiety. Among the most accessible mindfulness practices for Indian students are deep breathing exercises. These exercises involve slow, intentional breathing that triggers the body's relaxation response, thereby soothing the mind. Educators can implement deep breathing routines before examinations, during transitions between classes, or at the commencement of the school day to aid students in resetting and concentrating. Over time, students can independently employ deep breathing techniques to manage exam-related stress, social anxiety, and other forms of pressure.

Progressive muscle relaxation (PMR) represents another effective mindfulness strategy for Indian students. PMR entails systematically tensing and subsequently relaxing various muscle groups, which increases awareness of physical tension and facilitates its release. This method is particularly advantageous for students who experience physical tension prior to exams or presentations. Teachers can lead brief PMR sessions within the classroom, or students can practice it independently at home as part of their personal stress management regimen. This straightforward technique swiftly alleviates physical tension and induces a state of calmness.

Visualization is an additional mindfulness technique that proves effective in stress management. During visualization exercises, students are encouraged to imagine serene or positive scenarios, such as traversing a forest, sitting beside a tranquil lake, or successfully completing an exam. This mental imagery assists students in diverting their attention from stressors towards calming and uplifting thoughts. Educators can facilitate visualization sessions before examinations or during particularly stressful periods in the academic calendar, providing students with a mental respite and aiding them in refocusing on their objectives with increased calmness and confidence.

Effective time management is also integral to stress management for Indian students, who often balance academic responsibilities, extracurricular activities, and familial expectations. Mindfulness-based time management involves instructing students on how to prioritize tasks, decompose large assignments into manageable steps, and establish realistic goals. By helping students organize their time efficiently, educators can mitigate the stress associated with procrastination or last-minute exam preparation. Simple tools such as to-do lists, study schedules, and goal-setting exercises can be incorporated into classroom activities to enhance students' ability to manage their workloads effectively. This methodology not only reduces stress but also enhances academic performance by promoting a more structured approach to learning.

Journaling serves as another mindfulness tool that aids students in processing their emotions and managing stress. By documenting their feelings, students can gain insights into the sources of their stress and develop coping mechanisms to address them. Teachers can introduce reflective journaling as a classroom practice, encouraging students to articulate their thoughts and emotions following particularly challenging days or weeks. This practice enables students to externalize their stress, gain perspective, and identify strategies for emotional management. Furthermore, journaling fosters self-awareness and emotional regulation, which are critical for sustained emotional well-being.

In addition to mindfulness techniques, physical activity plays a vital role in stress management. Yoga, with its Indian origins, offers an effective means for students to alleviate stress while enhancing physical strength and flexibility. Schools can provide yoga classes or incorporate brief yoga sessions into the daily schedule, allowing students to stretch, breathe, and concentrate on their bodies. Even short yoga sessions can significantly reduce stress, improve concentration, and boost overall well-being. Many Indian schools have already begun integrating yoga into their physical education curricula, in line with the NEP 2020's emphasis on mental and physical health.

Educational institutions can also facilitate workshops or seminars on stress management techniques, wherein mental health professionals guide students through mindfulness practices and offer practical advice for handling academic pressures. These workshops may address topics such as managing exam stress, coping with failure, and balancing academic and personal life. By normalizing conversations about stress and mental health, schools can foster a more supportive environment where students feel comfortable seeking assistance when necessary.

Parental involvement is another essential element in helping students manage stress. Parents can reinforce mindfulness and stress management practices at home by encouraging their children to take breaks, engage in relaxation techniques, and maintain a healthy balance between academic and leisure activities. Schools can support this by providing parents with resources on how to bolster their children's emotional and mental well-being. For instance, schools can organize informational sessions for parents on the significance of mindfulness and stress management, ensuring that students receive consistent support both at home and in the educational setting.

The NEP 2020 underscores the necessity of a more holistic approach to education, recognizing that students' mental and emotional health is paramount to their academic achievement. By embedding mindfulness and stress management techniques within the school curriculum, Indian educational institutions can equip students with the skills required to navigate academic pressures and sustain their emotional health. These practices not only mitigate stress but also enhance students' ability to concentrate, remain composed under pressure, and approach challenges with a positive outlook.

7.8 Case Studies of Emotional Learning Success in India

Emotional learning programs have been successfully implemented across various schools in India, demonstrating the significant impact of Social-Emotional Learning (SEL) on student well-being, academic performance, and overall development. These case studies highlight how integrating emotional learning into the school curriculum fosters environments that support both academic success and mental health. The following examples illustrate different approaches to SEL and mindfulness in Indian schools, showcasing their benefits.

One exemplary case is the Municipal Corporation of Greater Mumbai (MCGM), which introduced SEL programs in several government-run schools through the "Jeevan Kaushal" initiative. This program aimed to equip students with essential life skills, including emotional regulation, self-awareness, and interpersonal communication. Utilizing activity-based learning, students engaged in role-playing, group discussions, and collaborative projects, which helped build empathy, resilience, and conflict-resolution abilities. Over time, teachers observed notable improvements in students' emotional responses, particularly in managing stress and peer conflicts. Additionally, attendance rates increased, and there was a marked rise in student engagement and motivation in academic activities.

Another significant example comes from a private school in Bangalore, where mindfulness and SEL were integrated into the curriculum. The school incorporated mindfulness practices such as focused breathing, guided meditation, and reflective journaling into the daily routine. Students participated in morning mindfulness sessions to begin the day with calmness and clarity, enhancing their focus in class. Teachers received SEL training, enabling them to embed emotional learning into their lessons effectively. Throughout the year, students reported lower anxiety levels during exams, and teachers noted improved classroom behavior, with students exhibiting greater patience, empathy, and cooperation. The success of this approach led to its adoption across all grade levels within the school.

These instances demonstrate the potential of SEL and mindfulness practices to transform educational settings in India. By fostering emotional intelligence and providing students with tools to manage stress and interpersonal relationships, schools can significantly enhance both academic outcomes and overall student well-being. The effective implementation of such programs reflects a growing recognition of the importance of holistic education, in line with broader educational policies advocating for the development of well-rounded individuals.

CHAPTER 8

INQUIRY-BASED AND DISCOVERY EARNING

8.1 Foundations of Inquiry-Based Learning for Indian Education

Inquiry-based learning (IBL) is a student-centered approach that encourages learners to ask questions, explore concepts, and actively engage in the learning process. Unlike traditional methods that focus on rote memorization, inquiry-based learning fosters critical thinking, creativity, and problem-solving by allowing students to take control of their learning. This approach is particularly relevant to the Indian education system, where there has been a growing recognition of the need to move away from exam-focused, teacher-directed instruction towards more dynamic and meaningful learning experiences.

The foundation of inquiry-based learning lies in the belief that students learn best when actively involved in the process of discovery. This approach aligns with the objectives of the National Education Policy (NEP) 2020, which highlights the importance of developing critical thinking and problem-solving abilities over rote learning. By encouraging students to ask questions, explore real-world issues, and reflect on their discoveries, inquiry-based learning helps students gain a deeper understanding of the subject matter, making learning more relevant and engaging.

In the Indian education system, inquiry-based learning can be particularly effective in addressing some of the key challenges it faces. Traditional teaching methods in India often emphasize standardized testing and content-heavy syllabi, which can lead to disengagement among students who find it difficult to see the relevance of what they are learning. Inquiry-based learning, on the other hand, enables students to explore topics they are interested in and encourages active participation, helping to re-engage learners and make education more meaningful.

A key principle of inquiry-based learning is that it is driven by students' curiosity and questions. Teachers act as facilitators, guiding students through the exploration and discovery process rather than being the sole providers of knowledge. This represents a significant shift in pedagogy, especially in Indian classrooms, where teacher-centered instruction has traditionally dominated. As more schools and educators embrace inquiry-based methods, students are gaining opportunities to develop critical thinking skills and apply their knowledge to real-life situations.

Inquiry-based learning also promotes interdisciplinary learning, where students can make connections between various subjects. For instance, a science lesson on environmental conservation might lead students to explore geography, economics, and social issues, helping them understand how different subjects are interconnected. This approach not only deepens students' understanding but also prepares them for the complex challenges they will encounter in the real world (Figure 8.1).

Additionally, inquiry-based learning encourages collaboration and communication, as students often work in groups to explore problems, share findings, and propose solutions. This collaborative approach is especially valuable in the Indian context, where teamwork and group dynamics are critical skills for success both academically and professionally. Through group work, students learn to listen to various perspectives, share ideas, and work together to solve problems, all of which contribute to the development of social and emotional skills.

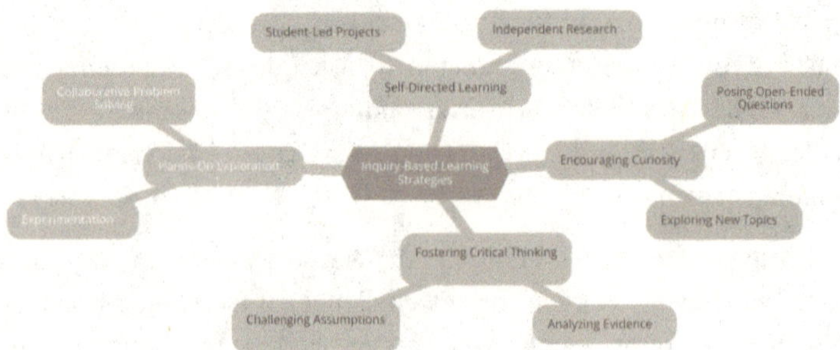

Figure 8.1: This mind map illustrates strategies for **Inquiry-Based Learning**, including:

- **Encouraging Curiosity**:
  o Posing open-ended questions and exploring new topics.
- **Fostering Critical Thinking**:
  o Analyzing evidence and challenging assumptions.
- **Hands-On Exploration**:
  o Experimentation and collaborative problem-solving.
- **Self-Directed Learning**:
  o Student-led projects and independent research.

The NEP 2020 supports the adoption of inquiry-based learning as part of its broader vision for a more holistic and learner-centric education system. By focusing on inquiry, the policy aims to create an education system that values creativity, critical thinking, and problem-solving, helping students develop the skills they need to thrive in the 21st century. This shift towards inquiry-based learning also aligns with global trends in education, where many countries are moving away from traditional methods in favor of approaches that encourage deeper engagement and active learning.

8.2 Encouraging Curiosity and Critical Thinking in Indian Schools

Fostering curiosity and critical thinking within Indian educational institutions is essential for equipping students to navigate future complexities. Traditionally, the Indian education system has prioritized rote memorization, often at the expense of creativity and independent reasoning. However, the National Education Policy (NEP) 2020 underscores the imperative to cultivate curiosity, inquiry, and critical thinking as fundamental educational pillars.

Curiosity serves as the catalyst for inquiry-based learning, encouraging students to pose questions, explore novel ideas, and investigate problems, thereby transforming them into active learners. In Indian classrooms, nurturing curiosity can be achieved by establishing an environment that values student inquiries and promotes exploration. For instance, educators might initiate lessons with open-ended questions that stimulate interest and provoke deeper contemplation of the subject matter. Allowing students the autonomy to delve into topics that intrigue them fosters a sense of curiosity, thereby enhancing their engagement and enthusiasm for learning.

Critical thinking, intrinsically linked to curiosity, involves the ability to analyze information, assess evidence, and draw reasoned conclusions. In a context where students are often required to absorb and reproduce extensive information, critical thinking skills are crucial for transcending rote memorization and engaging with content on a more profound level. Educators can cultivate critical thinking by encouraging students to challenge assumptions, consider alternative perspectives, and substantiate their conclusions with evidence. For example, in a history class, rather than solely memorizing dates and events, students might critically examine the causes and effects of specific events and debate their impacts from multiple viewpoints.

A pivotal strategy for enhancing curiosity and critical thinking in Indian schools is the establishment of a classroom culture that prioritizes inquiry over mere recall of information. This paradigm shift necessitates that educators move away from an exclusive focus on correct answers, instead promoting the exploration of diverse solutions to problems. Implementing inquiry-based learning methodologies, such as problem-based learning (PBL) or project-based learning, allows students to address real-world challenges collaboratively, encouraging them to apply their knowledge creatively and think innovatively alongside their peers.

Providing opportunities for independent exploration is equally important in promoting curiosity and critical thinking. The highly structured curricula prevalent in many Indian schools often leave little room for students to pursue their interests or engage in self-directed learning. To mitigate this, educators can incorporate inquiry-based projects that enable students to choose topics of personal interest and explore them comprehensively. For example, students might design their own scientific experiments, conduct independent research on societal issues, or develop presentations on subjects that spark their curiosity. These projects not only enhance critical thinking but also instill a sense of ownership over their educational journey.

Technology plays a significant role in fostering curiosity and critical thinking within Indian schools. Digital resources such as online research platforms, educational applications, and interactive simulations provide students with access to extensive information and diverse learning opportunities beyond the traditional classroom setting. For instance, students can utilize virtual laboratories to perform experiments, explore interactive maps in geography lessons, or participate in global discussions on contemporary issues. Integrating technology into the learning process enables educators to create more dynamic and engaging educational experiences that stimulate curiosity and encourage critical analysis.

Beyond classroom practices, school leadership and policy frameworks are crucial in promoting curiosity and critical thinking. The NEP 2020 advocates for a shift from exam-centric education towards more flexible, learner-centered environments. Schools can support this transition by offering interdisciplinary curricula, minimizing the emphasis on rote memorization in assessments, and providing teachers with professional development in inquiry-based and critical thinking pedagogies. Aligning school policies with these objectives facilitates the creation of a learning culture that values curiosity, creativity, and independent thought.

Collaboration among teachers, students, and parents is also vital in cultivating an environment that encourages curiosity and critical thinking. Parents can support inquiry-based activities at home by encouraging their children to ask questions and providing resources for independent exploration. Educators can engage with parents to highlight the importance of these skills, demonstrating how they contribute to students' long-term success. Through such collaboration, schools and families can establish a supportive framework that nurtures students' innate curiosity and enhances their critical thinking capabilities.

8.3 Discovery Learning in Science and Mathematics in India

Discovery learning represents an instructional methodology that prioritizes active student engagement through exploration, experimentation, and problem-solving. In disciplines such as science and mathematics, this approach enables students to construct their understanding by directly interacting with concepts in a hands-on, inquiry-driven manner. Within the Indian educational context, where traditional pedagogy often emphasizes memorization and rote learning, the integration of discovery learning into science and mathematics curricula offers a robust means to cultivate deeper comprehension, critical thinking, and a sustained enthusiasm for exploration.

In the realm of science education, discovery learning facilitates direct interaction with scientific principles through experiments and observations. Rather than passively absorbing information about scientific concepts, students are encouraged to actively explore these ideas by conducting experiments, making predictions, and testing hypotheses. For instance, instead of merely learning about photosynthesis from textbooks, students might engage in planting seeds and observing the effects of sunlight and water on plant growth, thereby independently uncovering the process of photosynthesis. This experiential approach reinforces theoretical knowledge by connecting it with tangible, practical experiences.

Indian classrooms, traditionally characterized by lecture-based and textbook-centric instruction in science, can greatly benefit from the adoption of discovery learning. This pedagogical shift promotes curiosity and active participation, rendering science education more interactive and enjoyable. Educators can facilitate this by providing opportunities for students to design experiments, investigate real-world issues, and explore scientific phenomena in contexts that resonate with their everyday experiences. For example, students might examine concepts such as gravity, electricity, or chemical reactions through relatable experiments or by constructing simple models, thereby reinforcing their understanding through practical application.

Similarly, discovery learning holds significant value in mathematics education by fostering a deeper grasp of abstract concepts. Rather than relying solely on the memorization of formulas or procedural instructions, students engaged in a discovery-based mathematics environment are encouraged to explore mathematical patterns, relationships, and problems autonomously. For example, students might investigate geometric shapes by measuring angles and uncovering their interrelationships or tackle real-world problems that necessitate creative mathematical reasoning. This approach enables students to transcend superficial understanding and achieve a more comprehensive and conceptual mastery of mathematics.

Moreover, discovery learning addresses a prevalent challenge in Indian education: mathematics anxiety. Many students in India experience apprehension towards mathematics due to its abstract nature and the high stakes associated with academic performance. By promoting an exploratory and experimental approach, discovery learning makes mathematics more accessible and less intimidating. Students are encouraged to experiment with numbers, explore patterns, and develop solutions in a supportive, low-pressure environment, thereby building confidence and mitigating the fear of failure. This method helps students perceive mathematics as an engaging and understandable subject, moving away from the constraints of rote memorization.

Both science and mathematics discovery learning align with the objectives of the National Education Policy (NEP) 2020, which advocates for experiential and hands-on learning. The NEP emphasizes the development of critical thinking, problem-solving, and creativity-skills inherently nurtured through discovery learning. By encouraging students to pose questions, explore solutions, and think independently, discovery learning supports the cultivation of these essential competencies.

The role of educators is pivotal in facilitating discovery learning within science and mathematics. Instead of serving merely as transmitters of knowledge, teachers act as facilitators who guide students through the exploration process, providing support and encouragement as they encounter new concepts. This transition shifts the teacher's role from a knowledge provider to a learning facilitator, fostering an environment where students feel comfortable making mistakes, asking questions, and exploring diverse approaches to problem-solving. For instance, in a mathematics classroom, a teacher might present a complex problem and allow students to collaboratively discover the solution through trial and error, rather than immediately supplying the necessary formulas.

Integrating technology into discovery learning can further enhance student experiences in science and mathematics. Digital tools such as interactive simulations, virtual laboratories, and educational applications offer students innovative ways to explore concepts. For example, virtual simulations enable students to conduct experiments that might be impractical in a traditional classroom setting, such as investigating climate change variables or modeling chemical reactions. Additionally, educational apps that gamify mathematical problem-solving can render abstract concepts more engaging and accessible, thereby supporting the discovery learning process.

Collaboration and communication are also integral to discovery learning, as students frequently work together to investigate problems, share findings, and discuss solutions. This collaborative approach is particularly beneficial in Indian classrooms, where peer learning can enhance understanding and foster diverse perspectives. Group projects, peer discussions, and hands-on activities provide opportunities for students to practice teamwork, communication, and critical thinking, all while deepening their comprehension of scientific and mathematical concepts.

8.4 Developing Inquiry-Based Lesson Plans for Indian Students

Developing inquiry-based lesson plans for Indian students necessitates a transition from traditional, teacher-centered methodologies to a more student-driven paradigm, where learning is propelled by curiosity, questioning, and exploration. Inquiry-based learning (IBL) operates on the premise that students acquire knowledge most effectively when they actively engage in discovering and constructing understanding, rather than passively receiving information. For educators in India, crafting effective inquiry-based lesson plans involves designing opportunities for students to participate in hands-on activities, investigate real-world problems, and collaborate with peers to devise solutions.

A fundamental initial step in formulating an inquiry-based lesson plan is the identification of a central question or problem that will steer the learning process. This question should be open-ended, facilitating exploration and allowing for multiple potential solutions. For instance, in a science lesson focused on water conservation, the guiding question might be, "How can we use water more efficiently in our local community?" Such a question prompts students to delve into the issue, research various strategies, and develop their own solutions, thereby enhancing critical thinking and problem-solving abilities.

Upon establishing the central question, educators can structure the lesson around the distinct phases of inquiry. A typical framework for inquiry-based learning encompasses the following stages: posing questions, conducting research, gathering evidence, analyzing data, and presenting findings. These stages provide students with a structured yet flexible pathway, allowing creativity in their approach to the problem. For example, in a social studies class, students might explore the impacts of urbanization on their local environment. They could begin by questioning how urbanization affects pollution levels, conduct research using local data sources, and present their conclusions through reports or presentations (Figure 8.2).

Inquiry-based lesson plans also highlight the significance of student collaboration. Collaborative work enables students to exchange ideas, learn from diverse perspectives, and address complex problems that might be too formidable to tackle individually. In Indian classrooms, where students typically engage in solitary study to prepare for examinations, group work cultivates teamwork, communication, and social skills. Educators can promote collaboration by assigning group projects, organizing peer discussions, or facilitating cooperative learning activities that require students to depend on one another to complete tasks. For instance, in a mathematics class, students might collaborate to solve a real-world problem, such as designing a budget for a school event or calculating the cost of constructing a playground.

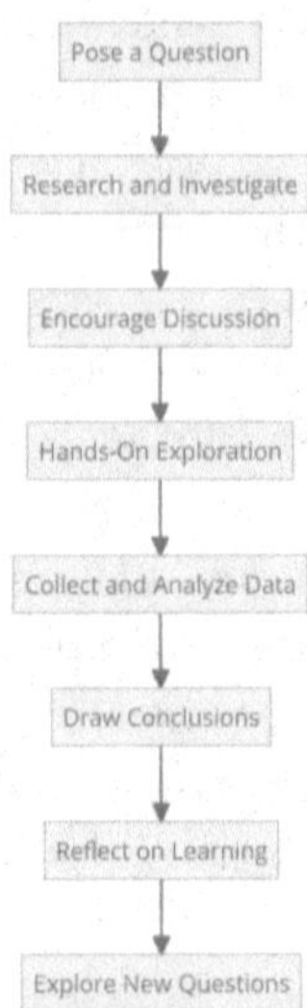

Figure 8.2: This diagram illustrates the structure of an **Inquiry-Based Lesson Plan**, starting from posing questions to exploring solutions:

1. **Pose a Question**: Begin by asking a thought-provoking question.

2. **Research and Investigate**: Encourage students to gather information.

3. **Encourage Discussion**: Facilitate discussion among students.

4. **Hands-On Exploration**: Engage students in hands-on activities to investigate.

5. **Collect and Analyze Data**: Gather data and analyze it for insights.

6. **Draw Conclusions**: Help students come to conclusions based on the evidence.

7. **Reflect on Learning**: Reflect on the learning outcomes.

8. **Explore New Questions**: Generate new questions based on the lesson.

Another fundamental aspect of inquiry-based lesson planning is the incorporation of interdisciplinary elements into the educational experience. Inquiry-based learning is inherently conducive to interdisciplinary teaching, enabling students to investigate connections across various domains of knowledge. For instance, in a module on sustainable agriculture, students might examine the scientific principles underlying crop rotation, evaluate the economic ramifications of diverse farming practices, and study the cultural traditions related to agriculture. This multifaceted approach not only enriches students' comprehension of the subject matter but also enhances the relevance and applicability of their learning to real-world contexts.

Technology is instrumental in augmenting inquiry-based lesson plans. Digital resources facilitate student research, peer collaboration, and the presentation of findings in innovative and engaging formats. For example, students may utilize online databases to collect information, engage in virtual experiments, or employ educational applications to model real-world challenges. In a geography class, Geographic Information System (GIS) software can be used to analyze maps and climate change data, while in a biology class, virtual laboratories can enable experiments that are otherwise difficult to conduct in a traditional classroom setting. The integration of technology in inquiry-based lessons not only boosts student engagement but also provides avenues for more profound exploration and understanding.

Assessment within inquiry-based learning frameworks is predominantly formative, occurring continuously throughout the learning journey rather than solely at the conclusion of a unit. Educators can implement a variety of assessment techniques, including observations, student reflections, peer feedback, and presentations, to evaluate student comprehension and advancement. For example, in a project-based inquiry session, teachers might assess students based on their contributions to group efforts, their capacity to formulate meaningful questions, and their approaches to problem-solving. This assessment strategy offers a comprehensive view of student learning, emphasizing both the final outcomes and the developmental processes and skills acquired during the inquiry.

Aligning with the National Education Policy (NEP) 2020, educators should prioritize the promotion of creativity, critical thinking, and problem-solving within their lesson plans, as these are pivotal objectives of the policy. The NEP advocates for a transition from rote memorization to experiential and inquiry-driven education, underscoring the significance of active student participation in the learning process. By designing lesson plans that center on inquiry, teachers can facilitate the cultivation of essential skills, including critical thinking, collaboration, and the application of knowledge to address real-world challenges.

8.5 Challenges and Solutions in Inquiry-Based Education in India

Implementing inquiry-based education in Indian schools encounters several challenges, primarily due to the traditional emphasis on rote learning, standardized testing, and a rigid curriculum. However, the benefits of inquiry-based learning (IBL)-including the development of critical thinking, problem-solving, and creativity-render it essential to address these obstacles. By identifying common challenges and exploring practical solutions, educational institutions can make significant progress in integrating IBL into the Indian education system.

A major challenge is the exam-oriented culture prevalent in India, where students are assessed based on their ability to memorize and reproduce information rather than demonstrating critical thinking or problem-solving skills. This focus on examinations can hinder teachers from adopting inquiry-based methods, as they may feel compelled to "teach to the test" to ensure high student performance. To overcome this, schools and policymakers must balance the importance of exams with the need for holistic learning. The National Education Policy (NEP) 2020 acknowledges this issue by advocating for competency-based assessments that evaluate students' ability to apply knowledge in real-world contexts, moving away from mere rote memorization.

Another related challenge is the rigidity of the current curriculum and the time constraints faced by teachers. The existing curriculum often allows little flexibility for incorporating inquiry-based learning, leading educators to feel that there is insufficient time to cover all required content while engaging students in inquiry-driven activities. One solution is to integrate inquiry-based learning within existing lessons rather than treating it as an additional task. For example, instead of solely lecturing on a historical event, a teacher might design a lesson where students investigate different perspectives on that event and present their findings. This approach enables teachers to cover the curriculum while simultaneously fostering critical thinking and exploration.

Resource limitations and inadequate infrastructure, particularly in rural areas, pose another significant barrier to implementing inquiry-based learning. IBL typically requires materials, technology, and spaces conducive to experimentation, which may be scarce in resource-poor schools. To address this, schools can adopt low-cost, resource-efficient strategies for inquiry-based learning. Teachers can utilize locally available materials for scientific experiments, encourage students to leverage community resources for research, or design projects that do not heavily rely on technology. Additionally, partnerships with local organizations, non-governmental organizations (NGOs), or government programs can provide access to resources that support inquiry-based education.

Teacher training represents a further challenge, as many Indian educators have been trained in traditional, teacher-centered methods and may be unfamiliar with the pedagogies required for inquiry-based education. Transitioning from the role of a knowledge provider to that of a facilitator can be uncomfortable for some teachers. Professional development programs are essential to equip teachers with the necessary skills and confidence to implement IBL effectively. Workshops, mentorship programs, and peer collaboration opportunities can assist teachers in designing inquiry-based lessons, managing student-led projects, and assessing inquiry-driven outcomes. The NEP 2020 emphasizes the importance of ongoing teacher training, particularly in areas like critical thinking and experiential learning, to ensure educators are prepared to adopt new educational practices.

Resistance to change from both students and parents constitutes another obstacle. Indian students are often accustomed to a structured, teacher-centered learning environment, and transitioning to an inquiry-based model, where students assume greater responsibility for their learning, can be unsettling. To address this, schools must involve both students and parents in the transition process by elucidating the benefits of inquiry-based learning. Hosting informational sessions for parents can demonstrate how inquiry promotes deeper understanding and equips students for real-world problem-solving. Additionally, teachers can introduce IBL gradually, allowing students to build confidence and familiarity with the approach over time.

8.6 Assessing Inquiry-Based Learning Outcomes in Indian Classrooms

Assessing the outcomes of inquiry-based learning (IBL) in Indian classrooms requires a shift from traditional evaluation methods, which focus on memorization and rote learning, to more holistic approaches that measure critical thinking, creativity, and problem-solving skills. Inquiry-based learning emphasizes discovery, exploration, and student-driven investigation, making it essential to assess not only the final product but also the journey students take to reach their conclusions. In India, where exams and standardized assessments are deeply ingrained in the education system, transitioning to a more nuanced form of assessment can be challenging, but it is vital for accurately measuring the true impact of IBL (Figure 8.3).

One of the key principles in assessing inquiry-based learning is placing more emphasis on the process rather than just the outcome. Traditional assessments often focus on whether students provide the correct answers. However, in IBL, the evaluation centers around how students approach a problem, gather information, and develop their solutions. Teachers can assess students' ability to formulate questions, conduct research, and critically analyze information. For example, in a science inquiry project, students might be evaluated on how well they designed their experiment, gathered and interpreted data, and drew conclusions-even if their final answer is not entirely accurate. This process-oriented assessment promotes deeper learning and values critical thinking over mere recall, ensuring that students are recognized for their problem-solving skills and inquiry abilities.

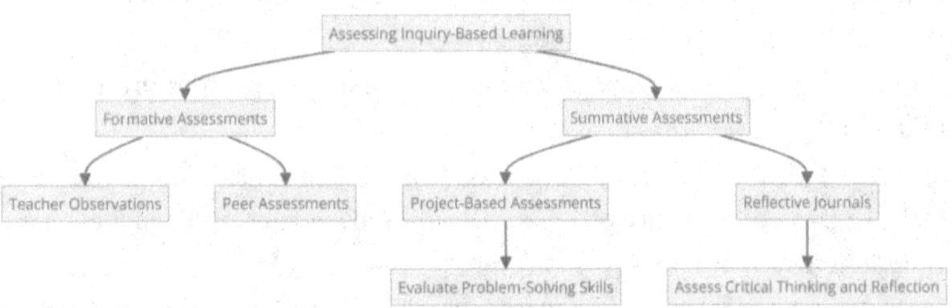

Figure 8.3: This flowchart shows methods to **Assess Inquiry-Based Learning Outcomes** in Indian classrooms:

1. **Formative Assessments**:
   o Teacher observations and peer assessments to gauge ongoing progress.
2. **Summative Assessments**:
   o Use project-based assessments and reflective journals to evaluate learning

outcomes.

    o **Evaluate Problem-Solving Skills**: Measure students' ability to solve complex problems.

    o **Assess Critical Thinking**: Analyze students' reflection and critical thinking through journaling.

Rubrics constitute an essential instrument for evaluating inquiry-based learning within Indian classrooms. A meticulously crafted rubric dissects the multifaceted components of inquiry-such as questioning, research, collaboration, and presentation-enabling educators to assess each dimension of a student's performance comprehensively. For instance, in a project focused on environmental sustainability, a rubric may encompass criteria like the thoroughness of research conducted, the innovativeness of proposed solutions, the efficacy of teamwork, and the lucidity of presentations. Employing rubrics allows teachers to establish clear expectations and provide constructive feedback, thereby assisting students in recognizing their strengths and identifying areas for improvement.

Beyond rubrics, formative assessments serve as an effective mechanism for gauging inquiry-based learning. These assessments occur continuously throughout the learning process, permitting educators to track student progress and deliver real-time feedback. Examples of formative assessments include classroom discussions, peer reviews, and reflective journals where students document their cognitive processes, challenges encountered, and insights gained during inquiry activities. For example, in a group project addressing local water conservation methods, students might maintain weekly reflections that detail their learning experiences, the evolution of their thinking, and the obstacles they faced. This ongoing assessment approach not only keeps students engaged with the material but also enables teachers to intervene promptly when students encounter difficulties.

Peer assessment is another valuable tool in the evaluation of inquiry-based learning. Given that collaboration and teamwork are integral to inquiry-based classrooms, peer assessments encourage students to appraise each other's contributions to group endeavors. This practice fosters accountability and self-awareness while enhancing students' abilities to provide and receive constructive feedback. Peer assessments might concentrate on aspects such as collaboration, the articulation of ideas, and contributions to problem-solving efforts, thereby allowing students to reflect on both their individual learning and that of their peers.

Presentations and portfolios also offer effective means of assessing outcomes from inquiry-based learning. Numerous inquiry projects necessitate that students present their findings to the class, either individually or in groups. Presentations enable students to articulate their thought processes, defend their conclusions, and respond to inquiries from peers or educators. This method of assessment evaluates not only the substance of their findings but also their communication skills, confidence, and capacity to engage an audience. Similarly, portfolios, which compile students' research, reflections, and final products, provide a holistic view of their learning trajectory. Portfolios allow students to demonstrate their progress over time and showcase the various stages of their inquiry journey, from initial questions to final conclusions.

In the Indian educational context, where examinations hold a pivotal role in student evaluation, integrating inquiry-based assessments with traditional exams can bridge the gap between these two approaches. For example, in subjects such as science or social studies, a portion of the final grade might derive from an inquiry project or presentation, while another segment could originate from written examinations. This hybrid approach preserves the structure of conventional exams while also acknowledging the critical thinking and problem-solving skills cultivated through inquiry-based learning. Additionally, incorporating inquiry-based questions into examinations-such as open-ended queries that require students to analyze data, establish connections, or propose solutions-can move the focus from mere information recall to deeper cognitive engagement.

The National Education Policy (NEP) 2020 advocates for a transition from high-stakes, rote-based assessments to more competency-based evaluations. This policy shift aligns with the tenets of inquiry-based learning by emphasizing the assessment of students' abilities to apply knowledge in practical, real-world scenarios. By adopting more flexible, process-oriented assessment approaches, Indian schools can better facilitate the development of essential 21st-century skills, including creativity, critical thinking, and collaboration.

8.7 Integrating Inquiry-Based Learning with Indian Education Policies

Integrating inquiry-based learning (IBL) with Indian education policies, particularly the National Education Policy (NEP) 2020, is crucial for aligning classroom practices with the nation's overarching educational objectives. The NEP 2020 advocates a transition from rote memorization to an education system that prioritizes creativity, critical thinking, problem-solving, and experiential learning-principles that are fundamental to inquiry-based learning. By embedding IBL within these policies, Indian schools can cultivate a more engaging and dynamic learning environment, equipping students to tackle the complexities of the 21st century.

A primary objective of the NEP 2020 is to transform the traditional, exam-centric education system into one that values holistic and student-centered learning. This objective directly corresponds with the tenets of inquiry-based learning, which encourage students to pose questions, explore concepts, and construct knowledge through investigation. Incorporating IBL into Indian education policies entails moving beyond a content-heavy curriculum to one that facilitates deeper subject exploration. For example, in a history lesson, rather than memorizing dates and events, students could examine the causes and consequences of historical occurrences using primary sources, fostering critical analysis and independent conclusions.

Successful integration of inquiry-based learning into Indian education necessitates the adoption of more flexible curricula that accommodate exploration and discovery. Traditionally, Indian curricula have been rigid, emphasizing the coverage of specific content within constrained timeframes. However, the NEP 2020 promotes a more interdisciplinary approach, enabling students to explore connections across subjects and engage in projects that require the application of knowledge across different domains. For instance, a project on climate change could incorporate elements of science, geography, and social studies, allowing students to investigate the issue from multiple perspectives. This interdisciplinary methodology not only enhances students' comprehension but also renders learning more pertinent to real-world challenges.

Another critical aspect of integrating IBL with Indian education policies involves shifting the focus of assessment from rote memorization to competency-based evaluations. The NEP 2020 underscores the necessity for assessments that measure students' ability to apply knowledge in practical, meaningful contexts. Inquiry-based learning facilitates this by encouraging the development of critical thinking, problem-solving, and research skills, which can be evaluated through projects, presentations, and collaborative work. For example, in a science class, students might be assessed on their ability to design and conduct experiments, interpret data, and present their findings, rather than solely recalling scientific facts.

Teacher training is paramount for the effective integration of inquiry-based learning with Indian education policies. Many educators in India have been trained in traditional, lecture-based methodologies and may lack familiarity with the pedagogies required for IBL. Transitioning from the role of a knowledge transmitter to that of a facilitator can be challenging for some teachers. The NEP 2020 advocates for continuous professional development to equip teachers with the skills necessary to implement more interactive and student-centered learning approaches. Workshops, seminars, and peer learning opportunities can aid teachers in designing inquiry-based lessons, managing student-led projects, and assessing inquiry-driven outcomes. Furthermore, schools can establish communities of practice where teachers collaborate and share strategies for incorporating IBL into their instructional practices.

The NEP 2020 also highlights the significance of experiential learning, which is closely aligned with inquiry-based learning. Experiential learning involves engaging students in hands-on, real-world experiences that enable them to apply their knowledge in practical contexts. This can encompass field trips, internships, or community projects where students investigate real-world problems and propose solutions. For example, students might collaborate with local environmental organizations to study water conservation efforts or participate in business internships to gain insights into entrepreneurship. By integrating experiential learning opportunities into the curriculum, schools can create more meaningful and engaging educational experiences that are in harmony with the objectives of IBL.

Technology plays a pivotal role in supporting the integration of inquiry-based learning with Indian education policies. The NEP 2020 acknowledges the importance of digital learning tools and advocates for their use to enhance education. Inquiry-based learning can be enriched through digital tools such as online research platforms, virtual simulations, and collaborative learning environments, which provide students with opportunities to explore concepts in greater depth and connect with peers beyond the classroom. For instance, students can utilize online databases for research on global issues, engage in virtual experiments, or collaborate with students from other schools on inquiry-based projects. The incorporation of technology into inquiry-based learning fosters more dynamic and interactive educational environments, preparing students for the digital era.

8.8 Case Studies of Inquiry-Based Learning in Indian Schools

Inquiry-based learning (IBL) has been effectively implemented in various Indian schools, demonstrating its capacity to transform classrooms into dynamic environments where students actively engage with content and develop critical thinking skills. These case studies illustrate the practical application of IBL across different regions and subjects, providing insights into how this approach can be tailored to the Indian educational context. From rural to urban settings, IBL has proven successful in fostering curiosity, problem-solving abilities, and collaborative skills among students.

A notable instance of IBL can be found in a government school in Delhi, where project-based learning (PBL), a variant of IBL, was introduced across multiple subjects. In one such project, students tackled the issue of air pollution in Delhi by investigating its causes, effects, and potential solutions. Under the guidance of their teachers, students conducted research, analyzed air quality data, and interviewed local experts to gain a comprehensive understanding of the problem. Collaborating in groups, they proposed solutions to reduce air pollution in their communities, such as promoting green spaces, lowering vehicle emissions, and increasing public awareness about pollution control measures. The project concluded with presentations to the school and local community, allowing students to share their findings and action plans. This initiative not only deepened students' grasp of the complexities surrounding air pollution but also enhanced their research and presentation skills.

In another case study, a private school in Bangalore integrated IBL into its science curriculum by focusing on ecosystems and biodiversity. Moving away from textbook-centric instruction, students were encouraged to explore their local environment and conduct field research. They visited nearby parks, nature reserves, and rivers to observe ecosystems in action, collecting data on various plant and animal species and studying the interactions between different organisms. After gathering their data, students analyzed their findings, compared them with existing scientific knowledge, and presented their conclusions. This hands-on approach facilitated a deeper understanding of ecological concepts and strengthened students' observational and analytical skills. The school reported increased student engagement and a heightened interest in environmental issues as a result of this inquiry-based project.

A rural school in Maharashtra offers another compelling example of IBL in practice. Partnering with a local non-governmental organization (NGO), the school introduced IBL into its social studies curriculum. Students were assigned to investigate the impact of water scarcity in their village and explore potential solutions to the problem. As part of the inquiry process, students interviewed local farmers, researched water conservation techniques, and studied government policies related to water management. Working collaboratively, they developed proposals to improve water usage in their community, including rainwater harvesting and the adoption of drought-resistant crops. This project not only educated students about the challenges of water management but also empowered them to actively participate in addressing a real-world issue affecting their community. It demonstrated how IBL can be adapted to rural contexts, enabling students to explore local challenges and devise practical solutions.

Furthermore, several schools across India have successfully incorporated IBL into their mathematics curricula. A case study from a school in Chennai highlights the use of IBL to teach mathematical concepts through real-world applications. In this school, students were presented with an open-ended geometry problem: designing a new playground for their school. To address this challenge, students applied their knowledge of shapes, measurements, and area calculations. Working in groups, they developed blueprints for the playground, calculated the materials and costs required for construction, and presented their designs to the school administration. This inquiry-based project allowed students to recognize the practical applications of geometry in their daily lives, making mathematics more relevant and engaging.

Another significant example comes from a school in Rajasthan that implemented IBL in its history lessons. Rather than relying on rote memorization of historical dates and events, students were encouraged to investigate the impact of historical figures on their region. They conducted research on local history, interviewed community elders, and analyzed primary sources such as letters, diaries, and photographs. This project enabled students to develop a deeper appreciation of their cultural heritage while honing their research and critical thinking skills. By engaging directly with historical sources and personal narratives, students gained a more nuanced and personal perspective on history.

CHAPTER 9

COLLABORATIVE AND COOPERATIVE LEARNING

9.1 The Benefits of Collaborative Learning in Indian Education

Collaborative learning constitutes an instructional methodology that emphasizes student interaction, cooperation, and shared accountability for educational outcomes. In the context of Indian education, where conventional classrooms frequently prioritize individual achievement and competition, this approach represents a significant shift towards fostering teamwork, problem-solving abilities, and peer support. By promoting collaborative efforts, project-based initiatives, and group discussions, collaborative learning cultivates essential social competencies, enhances academic performance, and fosters a more inclusive educational environment.

A primary advantage of collaborative learning lies in its capacity to deepen students' comprehension of subject matter. Through collaboration, students encounter diverse perspectives, facilitating the exploration of novel ideas and the development of a more comprehensive understanding of the topics under study. For example, in a collaborative science project, students with varying strengths and viewpoints engage in more substantive discussions and innovative problem-solving. In Indian classrooms, where the emphasis is often on memorization and the replication of information for examinations, collaborative learning provides an avenue to transcend rote learning and engage with material in a more meaningful and analytical manner.

Another significant benefit of collaborative learning is the enhancement of critical social and communication skills. Group work necessitates effective communication, active listening, and conflict resolution, all of which are vital for success in both academic and professional settings. In India, where there is considerable pressure for individual performance, collaborative learning shifts the focus from competition to cooperation. It imparts skills in idea sharing, constructive feedback, and peer support, thereby creating a more positive and collaborative classroom atmosphere.

Furthermore, collaborative learning contributes to the augmentation of students' confidence and self-esteem. Traditional classroom settings can lead to feelings of isolation or discouragement among students who struggle with certain subjects, especially if they are unable to keep pace with instruction.

Collaborative learning mitigates this by providing opportunities for mutual support, fostering a sense of belonging, and sharing responsibility for learning outcomes. For instance, a student proficient in mathematics might assist a peer facing difficulties, while the latter may offer strengths in areas such as creative thinking or presentation skills. This reciprocal support not only enhances students' confidence but also reinforces the notion that every individual possesses valuable contributions to offer.

Moreover, collaborative learning equips students with the skills necessary to meet the demands of the contemporary workforce. In an increasingly interconnected and globalized world, teamwork and collaboration are indispensable in virtually every profession. Through group activities and collaborative projects, students gain practical experience in working with others, navigating group dynamics, and managing shared responsibilities. This experiential learning not only bolsters academic performance but also endows students with teamwork and leadership abilities that are highly prized in professional environments. In Indian educational settings, where the focus traditionally lies on individual accomplishments, collaborative learning presents a vital opportunity for students to develop competencies that will facilitate their success in future careers.

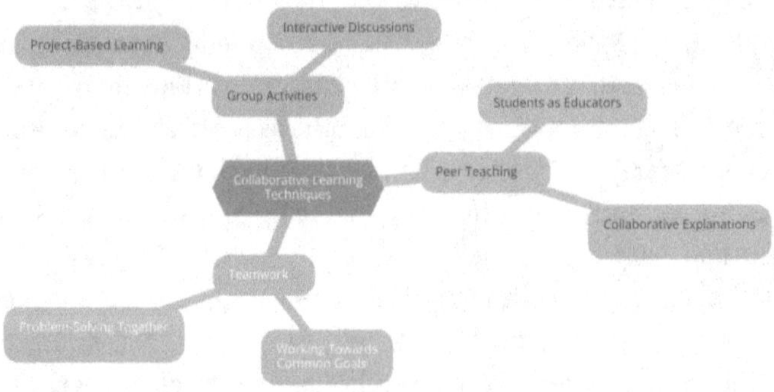

Figure 9.1: This mind map illustrates **Collaborative Learning Techniques**, including:

1. **Group Activities**:
   o Involves project-based learning and interactive discussions.
2. **Peer Teaching**:
   o Students take on the role of educators and explain concepts collaboratively.
3. **Teamwork**:
   o Focuses on working together towards common goals and solving problems

as a group.

The NEP 2020 emphasizes the importance of developing 21st-century skills such as critical thinking, problem-solving, and collaboration. Collaborative learning aligns perfectly with these goals, as it encourages students to think critically, solve problems as a team, and engage in meaningful discussions about the subjects they are studying. By integrating collaborative learning into the curriculum, Indian schools can create more dynamic and interactive classrooms where students are active participants in their learning.

9.2 Designing Group Activities for Effective Learning in Indian Schools

Collaborative learning constitutes a pedagogical approach that emphasizes student interaction, cooperation, and shared accountability in the educational process. In the Indian context, where conventional classrooms frequently prioritize individual achievement and competition, this methodology represents a significant shift towards fostering teamwork, problem-solving, and peer support. By promoting cooperative work, joint project endeavors, and participatory group discussions, collaborative learning cultivates essential social competencies, enhances academic performance, and contributes to a more inclusive educational environment.

A principal advantage of collaborative learning lies in its capacity to deepen students' comprehension of subject matter. Through collaboration, students encounter diverse perspectives, facilitating the exploration of novel ideas and the development of a more comprehensive understanding of their studies. For example, in a collaborative science project, students with varying strengths and viewpoints engage in more substantive discussions and innovative problem-solving activities. In Indian classrooms, where the emphasis often resides in memorizing facts and regurgitating information for examinations, collaborative learning provides an avenue to transcend rote learning and engage more profoundly with educational content.

Furthermore, collaborative learning significantly contributes to the development of critical social and communication skills. Group work necessitates effective communication, active listening, and conflict resolution, all of which are indispensable for success in both academic and professional settings. In India, where students frequently face pressure to excel individually, collaborative learning facilitates a transition from a competitive to a cooperative focus. It instructs students in the art of idea sharing, providing constructive feedback, and supporting peers, thereby fostering a more positive and collaborative classroom atmosphere.

Additionally, collaborative learning enhances students' confidence and self-esteem. In traditional educational settings, students who struggle with particular subjects may experience feelings of isolation or discouragement, especially if they are unable to keep pace with instructional demands. Collaborative learning offers a platform for mutual support, nurturing a sense of belonging and collective responsibility for learning. For instance, a student proficient in mathematics may assist a peer facing difficulties, while the latter contributes in areas such as creative thinking or presentation skills. This reciprocal support not only bolsters students' confidence but also reinforces the notion that each individual possesses valuable contributions.

Moreover, collaborative learning equips students with skills essential for the contemporary workforce. In an increasingly interconnected and globalized environment, teamwork and collaboration are pivotal across virtually all professions. Through group activities and collaborative projects, students gain practical experience in working alongside others, navigating group dynamics, and managing shared responsibilities. This experiential learning not only augments their academic performance but also imparts teamwork and leadership abilities highly esteemed in professional contexts. In Indian schools, where individual performance is often emphasized, collaborative learning provides a critical opportunity for students to develop competencies that will facilitate their success in future careers.

9.3 Building Teamwork and Communication Skills in Indian Students

Building teamwork and communication skills in Indian students is pivotal for fostering academic excellence and preparing them for future professional environments. Within an education system traditionally centered on individual achievement and examination performance, there is an increasing acknowledgment of the necessity for collaboration and interpersonal competencies. Teamwork and communication are integral to enhancing group dynamics in classrooms and equipping students with the collaborative skills essential in today's workforce.

Teamwork involves students collaborating to achieve common objectives, facilitating the sharing of responsibilities, leveraging individual strengths, and collectively addressing challenges. In Indian educational settings, where individual work is often emphasized, introducing activities that require teamwork can help students recognize that success is contingent not only on personal effort but also on cooperative engagement. For instance, group projects in subjects such as science or social studies enable students to allocate tasks, collaborate effectively, and integrate their individual contributions into a cohesive final outcome.

Effective communication is fundamental to successful teamwork. In collaborative environments, students must articulate their ideas clearly, listen attentively to others, and provide constructive feedback. This aspect is particularly pertinent in Indian classrooms, where traditional hierarchical structures may inhibit students from openly sharing their opinions. Educators can foster an atmosphere where students feel comfortable contributing, posing questions, and expressing their viewpoints. Techniques such as group discussions or debates can encourage students to practice conveying their ideas and engaging respectfully with diverse perspectives.

Structured group activities serve as effective methods for cultivating teamwork skills. For example, in a mathematics class, students might be tasked with solving a complex problem collectively, with each member responsible for different segments of the equation. By distributing tasks within the group, students depend on each other's contributions to derive the correct solution. This approach not only enhances academic proficiency but also reinforces the importance of teamwork, as each member's input is vital to the group's overall success.

Role-playing exercises also prove to be potent means of developing communication skills. By assigning specific roles, students collaborate to achieve designated goals. In a business studies class, for instance, students could role-play as members of a marketing team, assuming roles such as project manager, market researcher, or content creator. These exercises enable students to practice communication, negotiation, and decision-making, while simultaneously fostering leadership and problem-solving abilities within real-world contexts, thereby further enhancing their teamwork and communication proficiencies.

Educators play a crucial role in facilitating the development of teamwork and communication skills. By exemplifying effective communication, active listening, and conflict resolution, teachers set a standard for students to emulate. For example, when mediating group discussions or resolving conflicts, educators can demonstrate how to listen to varying viewpoints, maintain composure under pressure, and identify common ground. Additionally, teachers can offer guidance on providing constructive feedback and encourage students to maintain respect when both giving and receiving criticism.

Integrating technology into group activities can further bolster teamwork and communication skills in Indian schools. Digital tools such as collaborative platforms, online forums, and educational applications enable students to collaborate in innovative manners. For instance, students can utilize online documents for joint research projects or engage in virtual discussions on various topics. These tools not only facilitate collaboration but also aid students in developing digital communication skills, which are increasingly important in the modern workforce. In institutions with limited technological resources, simpler tools like group messaging applications can still support communication and teamwork outside the traditional classroom setting.

Assessment plays a critical role in the cultivation of teamwork and communication skills. Beyond evaluating the academic outcomes of group work, educators should assess the effectiveness of student collaboration and communication. This can involve observing how students listen to one another, resolve conflicts, and work collectively to achieve shared goals. Peer assessment can also be beneficial, enabling students to reflect on their own contributions and provide feedback to their teammates. Following the completion of a group project, students might evaluate their peers' participation and offer suggestions for improvement, thereby fostering a reflective process that promotes personal growth in teamwork and communication.

The development of teamwork and communication skills aligns with the objectives of the National Education Policy (NEP) 2020, which underscores the importance of cultivating social and emotional competencies. The NEP advocates for educational institutions to transcend rote learning and create opportunities for collaborative, experiential learning. By fostering these skills, schools aid students in developing the interpersonal abilities that are crucial for both academic and professional success.

9.4 Assessing Group Work and Collaboration in Indian Classrooms

Assessing group work and collaboration in Indian classrooms is essential to ensure that students are not only achieving academic success but also developing the critical skills of teamwork, communication, and cooperation. In collaborative learning environments, students work together to solve problems, share ideas, and complete projects. To properly evaluate these interactions, teachers need to look beyond traditional assessments that focus solely on individual outcomes and instead consider how effectively students work as a team **(Figure 9.2)**.

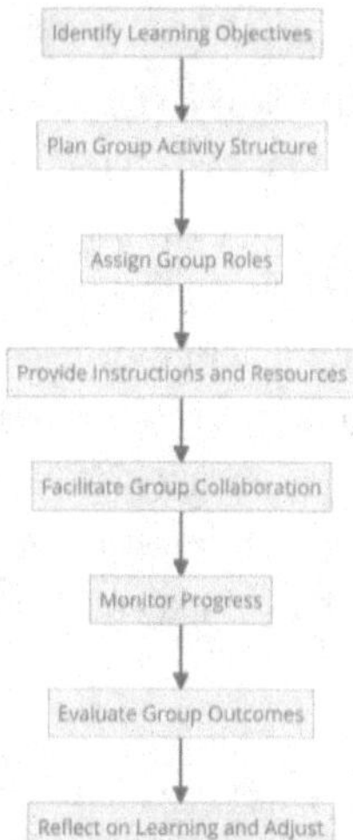

Figure 9.2: This flowchart depicts the steps for **Designing Effective Group Activities** in collaborative learning environments:

1. **Identify Learning Objectives**: Define clear goals for the group activity.
2. **Plan Group Activity Structure**: Design the structure of the activity.
3. **Assign Group Roles**: Distribute roles and responsibilities.
4. **Provide Instructions and Resources**: Ensure students have what they need to succeed.
5. **Facilitate Group Collaboration**: Support collaboration among group members.
6. **Monitor Progress**: Track the activity's progress.
7. **Evaluate Group Outcomes**: Assess the results of the group work.

Reflect on Learning and Adjust: Reflect on the learning outcomes and make adjustments for improvement.

One of the fundamental principles in assessing group work is the recognition of both the final product and the collaborative process. While evaluating the end result of a group project, such as a presentation or a written report, remains important, the dynamics of collaboration are equally significant. Assessing how students communicate, contribute to discussions, share responsibilities, and resolve conflicts offers a more comprehensive understanding of their collaborative abilities. For instance, in a science class where students collaborate on a laboratory experiment, educators might evaluate not only the accuracy of the experimental results but also how effectively students divided tasks, supported each other's efforts, and communicated their findings within the group.

To effectively assess group work, educators can employ rubrics that emphasize specific collaboration criteria. These rubrics may encompass categories such as communication, teamwork, problem-solving, and individual contributions. For example, a rubric designed for a social studies group project might assess how well students listened to each other's ideas, distributed the workload, and demonstrated mutual respect during discussions. By providing explicit criteria for assessment, rubrics clarify expectations for students and facilitate constructive feedback, enabling students to discern their strengths and identify areas for improvement. This method ensures accountability for participation and encourages students to actively contribute to the group's success.

Peer assessment constitutes another valuable tool for evaluating group work in Indian classrooms. In peer assessments, students evaluate their teammates' contributions to the group project and reflect on their own performance. This practice not only enhances self-awareness but also prompts students to consider the impact of their actions on the group's overall success. For example, after completing a group project, students might complete a peer assessment form rating their teammates on aspects such as participation, communication, and cooperation. Peer feedback is particularly useful in identifying imbalances within the group, such as when one student undertakes the majority of the work while others contribute less. Incorporating peer assessment provides educators with additional insights into group dynamics and allows them to address any emerging issues.

Self-assessment serves as another method to encourage students to reflect on their collaboration skills. Upon completing a group project, students can evaluate their own contributions and identify areas for improvement. For instance, a student might assess how effectively they communicated their ideas to the group or whether they actively listened to their peers' suggestions. Self-assessment fosters personal accountability and empowers students to take ownership of their roles within the group. In Indian classrooms, where the focus is often on individual performance, self-assessment shifts attention to the importance of collaboration and teamwork.

Formative assessments play a crucial role in monitoring group work throughout the project, rather than solely evaluating the final outcome. These assessments enable educators to observe the group's progress, provide timely feedback, and intervene when necessary to ensure effective functioning. For example, during a group project in a mathematics class, a teacher might periodically check in with each group to assess how well they are collaborating, whether they are sharing responsibilities, and how they are advancing toward their objectives. Real-time feedback from formative assessments assists students in refining their collaboration skills and keeps the group aligned with their goals.

In addition to rubrics, peer assessments, and formative assessments, presentations and reflective discussions are effective methods for assessing group work outcomes. Presentations allow students to demonstrate their collective efforts and illustrate how they collaborated to achieve their objectives. During presentations, educators can assess not only the content but also how well the group worked together to prepare and deliver their findings. Following presentations, reflective discussions enable students to articulate the challenges they faced as a group, the strategies they employed to resolve conflicts, and the lessons learned from the collaborative process. These discussions provide valuable insights into group dynamics and enhance students' understanding of effective teamwork.

When assessing group work, it is essential to recognize individual contributions to ensure that each student is acknowledged for their efforts. In scenarios where certain students assume more responsibility or contribute more significantly to the project, educators can evaluate both the group's overall performance and each student's individual contributions. For instance, a group might receive a collective grade for the final product, while each member is also assessed individually based on their participation, effort, and specific contributions. This dual assessment approach ensures that students are held accountable for their roles while simultaneously emphasizing the value of collaboration.

Technology can further facilitate the assessment of group work and collaboration. Digital tools such as collaborative platforms, online discussion boards, and shared documents enable educators to monitor how students communicate and cooperate. For example, in a group project utilizing Google Docs, teachers can track each student's contributions to the document, observe interactions in the comments section, and provide feedback directly on the platform. These tools streamline the assessment of the collaborative process and ensure that all students are actively contributing to the group's endeavors.

9.5 Technology Tools for Collaborative Learning in India

Incorporating technological tools into collaborative learning has significantly transformed India's educational landscape, offering students innovative methods to collaborate, exchange ideas, and address challenges. As technology becomes increasingly accessible, including in remote regions, educational institutions are investigating how digital platforms and tools can enhance classroom collaboration. The integration of technology into group activities enables students to participate in more dynamic and interactive learning experiences, surpassing the constraints of traditional group work.

A prominent technology tool facilitating collaborative learning in Indian classrooms is Google Workspace for Education, which encompasses applications such as Google Docs, Google Sheets, and Google Slides. These tools permit students to collaborate in real-time, jointly working on documents, presentations, and spreadsheets from diverse locations. For example, during a group research project, students can utilize Google Docs to co-author a report, with each member contributing distinct sections and providing feedback on their peers' inputs. Educators can simultaneously monitor the project's progress, offer recommendations, and evaluate individual contributions. This form of real-time collaboration is especially beneficial in Indian schools where students may have differing schedules and varying access to in-person group meetings.

Another widely adopted tool is Microsoft Teams, which enhances communication and collaboration among students and educators through features like chat, video conferencing, and shared documents. In Indian classrooms, Microsoft Teams can facilitate group discussions, resource sharing, and virtual meetings. For instance, students engaged in a science project might use Teams to conduct virtual brainstorming sessions, allocate tasks, and track their progress via shared files and updates. This level of connectivity strengthens teamwork, particularly in scenarios where face-to-face collaboration is impractical, such as during the COVID-19 pandemic or in rural areas with limited infrastructure.

By integrating these technological tools into educational settings, Indian educators can cultivate a more interactive and engaging learning environment. This empowerment allows students to take greater ownership of their learning processes, collaborate efficiently, and develop essential digital competencies. Furthermore, these tools can bridge geographical disparities, ensuring equitable participation in collaborative projects regardless of students' locations or circumstances. The utilization of such platforms not only fosters collaboration but also equips students with the teamwork and communication skills imperative for success in the contemporary digital workplace.

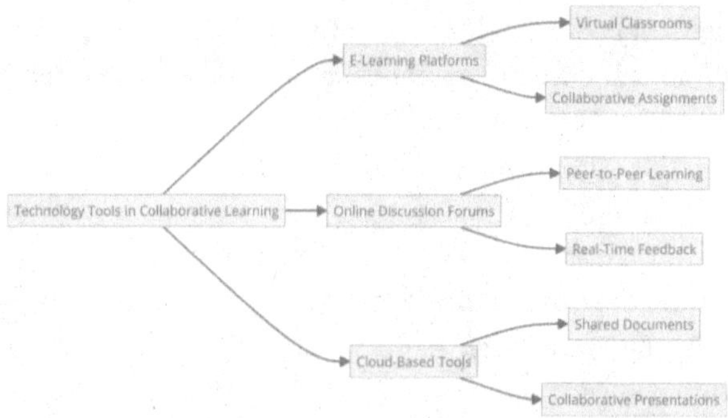

Figure 9.3: This diagram shows the use of **Technology Tools in Collaborative Learning** in Indian classrooms:

1. **E-Learning Platforms:**
   o Includes virtual classrooms and collaborative assignments.
2. **Online Discussion Forums:**
   o Promotes peer-to-peer learning and provides real-time feedback.
3. **Cloud-Based Tools:**
   o Enables shared documents and collaborative presentations.

Incorporating technological tools into collaborative learning has significantly transformed the educational landscape in India, offering students innovative avenues to collaborate, exchange ideas, and solve problems. As technology becomes increasingly accessible, including in remote areas, educational institutions are exploring how digital platforms and tools can enhance classroom collaboration. The integration of technology into group activities enables students to engage in more dynamic and interactive learning experiences, surpassing the limitations inherent in traditional group work.

A prominent example of such technological integration is Google Workspace for Education, which includes applications like Google Docs, Google Sheets, and Google Slides. These tools facilitate real-time collaboration, allowing students to work collectively on documents, presentations, and spreadsheets from disparate locations. In practice, a group research project might utilize Google Docs for co-authoring a report, with each member contributing distinct sections and providing feedback on their peers' work. Educators can monitor the project's progression, offer suggestions, and assess individual contributions effectively. This real-time collaborative capability is particularly advantageous in Indian schools where students may have varying schedules and limited opportunities for in-person group meetings.

Microsoft Teams is another widely adopted platform that enhances communication and collaboration among students and educators through features such as chat, video conferencing, and shared documents. In Indian classrooms, Microsoft Teams can facilitate group discussions, resource sharing, and virtual meetings. For instance, students engaged in a science project could utilize Teams to conduct virtual brainstorming sessions, allocate tasks, and monitor their progress through shared files and updates. This level of connectivity strengthens teamwork, especially in circumstances where in-person collaboration is unfeasible, such as during the COVID-19 pandemic or in rural areas with limited infrastructure.

Educational applications and platforms like Padlet and Jamboard further augment collaborative learning by providing interactive, virtual workspaces for brainstorming, research, and project development. These tools enable students to create and share content visually, making them ideal for projects that require creative thinking or problem-solving. For example, in a social studies class, students can employ Padlet to construct a shared board where they post articles, videos, and images related to a historical event under study. By visually organizing their research, students can identify connections between different sources and ideas, fostering a deeper understanding and more effective collaboration.

Learning management systems (LMS) such as Moodle and Edmodo offer comprehensive platforms for collaborative learning by incorporating features like discussion forums, group assignments, and peer feedback. In an Indian classroom utilizing an LMS, students might engage in class-wide discussions about a novel, contribute to a group assignment analyzing the book's themes, and provide peer feedback on each other's work. This structure facilitates a blend of independent and collaborative learning, aiding students in developing both critical thinking and teamwork skills.

Video conferencing platforms like Zoom and Google Meet have become indispensable for collaborative learning, particularly within remote or hybrid education models. These platforms enable students to participate in virtual group meetings, presentations, and discussions irrespective of their physical locations. For instance, students collaborating on a science experiment can conduct virtual meetings to discuss hypotheses, share findings, and plan subsequent steps. Additionally, video conferencing tools allow teachers to provide guidance and feedback throughout the collaboration process, ensuring that students remain focused and achieve their learning objectives.

In regions with limited access to advanced technology, mobile-based learning applications such as WhatsApp and Telegram offer viable alternatives for collaborative learning. In many parts of India, where internet access is predominantly through mobile devices, these apps provide accessible platforms for communication and collaboration. Students can create group chats to share ideas, distribute resources, and update each other on the progress of group projects. WhatsApp, for example, allows the exchange of documents, photographs, and voice messages, rendering it a flexible tool for collaboration in resource-constrained environments.

A significant advantage of utilizing technology tools in collaborative learning is the ability to track and assess individual contributions. Platforms like Google Docs and Microsoft Teams enable educators to monitor each student's input to a group project, facilitating the assessment of individual involvement and participation. This feature is particularly beneficial in Indian classrooms where evaluating group work can be challenging due to uneven participation. By leveraging technology, teachers can ensure accountability and provide targeted feedback to students who may require additional support.

Moreover, technology tools facilitate collaboration across geographical boundaries. In India, where students from rural areas may have limited access to resources or diverse perspectives, online collaboration tools enable connections with peers from different regions, cultures, and backgrounds. For example, a rural school might collaborate with an urban school on a joint project, allowing students to exchange ideas and learn from each other's experiences. This cross-cultural collaboration enriches the learning experience and exposes students to diverse ways of thinking.

The integration of technology into collaborative learning aligns with the objectives of the National Education Policy (NEP) 2020, which emphasizes the utilization of digital tools and resources to enhance education. The NEP underscores the importance of fostering 21st-century skills such as collaboration, digital literacy, and problem-solving, all of which are supported by the use of technology in group activities. By incorporating technology into collaborative learning, Indian schools can create more interactive, engaging, and effective learning environments, thereby preparing students for the demands of the modern workforce.

9.6 Teacher's Role in Facilitating Cooperative Learning in India

In cooperative learning environments, teachers assume a central role in guiding, structuring, and facilitating group interactions to ensure students gain the full benefits of collaborative work. In India, where traditional classrooms have often focused on teacher-centered instruction and individual performance, transitioning to cooperative learning requires educators to adopt strategies that foster teamwork, communication, and shared responsibility among students. By acting as facilitators, teachers can establish a classroom culture that values collaboration, promotes active participation, and supports the development of essential academic and life skills.

A fundamental responsibility of teachers in cooperative learning is designing structured opportunities for group work. Unlike traditional teaching methods that prioritize content delivery, cooperative learning emphasizes active student engagement in achieving shared goals. Teachers must develop group activities aligned with learning objectives, offering tasks that necessitate collaboration and critical thinking. For example, a science teacher might assign a project on renewable energy where teams research energy sources, conduct experiments, and present findings to the class. The teacher ensures the tasks are challenging yet achievable, fostering both cooperation and intellectual growth.

Establishing clear expectations and guidelines for group interactions is another critical aspect of the teacher's role. In many Indian classrooms, students may lack familiarity with teamwork, which can result in unequal participation or off-task behavior. Teachers can address these issues by defining roles and responsibilities within groups, such as assigning students to be leaders, note-takers, or presenters. Guidelines for respectful communication, such as active listening, taking turns, and providing constructive feedback, further ensure productive collaboration. By setting these expectations, teachers create an environment where every student contributes meaningfully to group tasks.

Monitoring and guiding group interactions is essential to maintaining the effectiveness of cooperative learning. Teachers act as facilitators, observing group dynamics, providing feedback, and intervening as needed. For instance, if one student dominates the discussion while others remain silent, the teacher might encourage quieter students to share their perspectives. Similarly, if a group encounters difficulties with a specific task, the teacher can suggest strategies or provide clarification to help them progress. This active involvement ensures equitable participation and keeps groups focused on their objectives.

Promoting inclusivity within group work is a vital responsibility, especially in Indian classrooms characterized by cultural, linguistic, and socio-economic diversity. Some students may feel hesitant to contribute due to language barriers or lack of confidence in their academic abilities. Teachers can foster an inclusive environment by modeling behaviors that value diverse perspectives and creating a safe space for students to express their ideas without fear of judgment. Strategies such as peer support, where students help one another navigate challenges, further enhance inclusivity and collaboration.

Teaching and reinforcing social and communication skills are integral to successful cooperative learning. Effective teamwork requires students to develop skills like active listening, conflict resolution, and negotiation. Teachers can integrate mini-lessons on these skills into the curriculum, equipping students with tools for managing group dynamics. For example, a teacher might demonstrate the use of "I" statements for conflict resolution or teach active listening techniques, such as paraphrasing a peer's comments. By imparting these skills, teachers ensure that students are better prepared to collaborate constructively.

Formative assessment provides teachers with a means to evaluate and enhance students' collaboration skills. By observing group interactions and offering timely feedback, teachers can highlight strengths and identify areas for improvement. For instance, after a history group project, a teacher might commend the group's research efforts while suggesting ways to improve their communication during presentations. Formative feedback encourages self-reflection and helps students understand how their individual contributions affect group success.

9.7 Challenges of Implementing Collaborative Learning in Indian Schools

Implementing collaborative learning in Indian schools presents significant benefits but is accompanied by a unique set of challenges. Traditional educational practices in India have long emphasized individual performance, rote memorization, and exam results, creating a competitive culture that often undermines cooperative approaches. Transitioning to collaborative learning, which prioritizes teamwork, problem-solving, and shared responsibility, requires a fundamental shift in teaching methods, classroom dynamics, and societal attitudes. Addressing these challenges is essential for the effective integration of collaborative learning into Indian classrooms.

A major hurdle is the entrenched focus on individual achievement. Indian students are accustomed to competing with peers for academic recognition, making it difficult to adapt to group settings where success hinges on collective effort. Collaborative learning requires students to share responsibilities, contribute to group tasks, and support each other's progress-a stark contrast to the prevailing competitive mindset. Resistance to this shift may stem from discomfort in relying on peers or reluctance to share credit for success.

Overcoming this barrier demands a cultural redefinition of success that values cooperation alongside individual excellence.

Teacher training and support are critical yet often insufficient in enabling the transition to collaborative learning. Many Indian educators are trained in traditional, lecture-based methodologies and may lack the skills or confidence to facilitate group activities effectively. Collaborative learning necessitates that teachers act as facilitators, guiding students in group interactions, resolving conflicts, and fostering communication. Without adequate professional development, teachers may revert to familiar teacher-centered methods. To address this, institutions must invest in training programs that equip teachers with strategies for implementing collaborative learning, managing diverse classroom dynamics, and leveraging technology to support group work.

Large class sizes in many Indian schools, particularly government-run institutions, pose another challenge. Managing group activities in crowded classrooms can lead to uneven participation, with some students being excluded or struggling to engage. Teachers may find it challenging to monitor group dynamics, provide feedback, or address conflicts effectively. Strategies such as dividing students into smaller groups, rotating among groups for guidance, and appointing peer leaders to oversee group tasks can help mitigate these difficulties and ensure equitable participation.

Resource limitations, especially in rural schools, further complicate the adoption of collaborative learning. Access to materials, technology, and flexible spaces necessary for group work is often restricted. In these settings, teachers may need to rely on resource-efficient methods, such as using locally available materials, encouraging creativity, and designing low-cost activities that promote teamwork. Partnering with NGOs, local businesses, or government programs can provide additional resources and support for collaborative initiatives, bridging the gap between resource availability and educational innovation.

India's cultural diversity adds complexity to implementing collaborative learning. Classrooms often encompass students from varied linguistic, cultural, and socio-economic backgrounds, which can create communication barriers and group dynamics issues. Students from marginalized communities may feel excluded, and language differences can hinder effective interaction. Teachers must foster inclusivity by strategically grouping students to ensure representation, offering language support, and cultivating a respectful classroom environment. Emphasizing respect for diverse perspectives and promoting peer support can transform this diversity into a strength, enriching the collaborative experience.

Time constraints and content-heavy curricula present further obstacles. The Indian education system's emphasis on covering extensive syllabi for standardized exams often leaves little room for collaborative or exploratory learning. Teachers may feel pressured to prioritize content delivery over process-oriented activities. Integrating collaborative tasks into existing lessons, where they deepen understanding of core concepts rather than replacing traditional instruction, can address this issue. Collaborative activities should complement and enhance the curriculum, enabling students to develop critical thinking and teamwork skills alongside academic knowledge.

9.8 Indian Case Studies: Successful Collaborative Learning Projects

Collaborative learning projects have demonstrated significant potential for fostering critical thinking, teamwork, and problem-solving skills in diverse educational contexts across India. From urban private institutions to rural government schools, these initiatives underscore the adaptability and effectiveness of cooperative educational approaches. Students engaged in such projects gain both academic proficiency and essential interpersonal skills critical for addressing future challenges.

The Riverside School in Ahmedabad exemplifies the integration of experiential learning through group initiatives emphasizing community impact. In one instance, students collaboratively designed environmental interventions addressing waste management, water conservation, and air pollution. Following comprehensive research, teams developed actionable solutions, including recycling programs and awareness campaigns. Engagement with local stakeholders facilitated practical feedback, reinforcing skills in communication and applied problem-solving alongside environmental literacy.

In a government school in rural Maharashtra, collaborative efforts targeted literacy improvement through student-created storybooks. Groups undertook roles as writers, illustrators, and editors, producing materials shared with younger peers. This approach not only enhanced literacy but also cultivated teamwork and creativity in a resource-constrained setting, demonstrating the adaptability of collaborative learning in addressing local educational needs.

A science curriculum initiative in Bangalore focused on renewable energy applications, tasking groups with investigating energy sources such as solar, wind, and hydropower. Teams developed functional models, including solar-powered water heaters and wind turbines, culminating in a science fair presentation. This project highlighted the value of collaborative inquiry in deepening conceptual understanding and fostering innovation in addressing scientific challenges.

A public school in Delhi implemented collaborative learning in a social studies context, requiring teams to design sustainable city models incorporating renewable energy, public transport, and green spaces. Through structured roles and the use of digital tools, students engaged in collective research and model construction, gaining practical experience in urban planning and collaborative decision-making.

These examples illustrate the efficacy of collaborative learning in diverse settings, emphasizing the development of academic and interpersonal competencies. By engaging students in cooperative projects, Indian schools are aligning with pedagogical strategies that prioritize holistic skill development.

CHAPTER 10

THE FUTURE OF TEACHING IN INDIA

10.1 Emerging Trends in Indian Education

The Indian education system is experiencing transformative changes, driven by emerging trends and innovations that are reshaping learning and teaching practices. These developments reflect global shifts in education alongside domestic efforts to modernize and prepare students for 21st-century challenges. Key trends are already influencing the system significantly and are poised to define the future of education in India.

One of the most prominent trends is the integration of technology into the educational landscape. Digital tools, online platforms, and mobile applications are becoming integral to classrooms, enhancing accessibility and engagement. From urban smart classrooms to rural areas leveraging mobile internet for lessons, technology is bridging gaps in access and quality. The COVID-19 pandemic accelerated this transition, making online learning a necessity during school closures. As schools reopen, blended learning models-combining traditional teaching with digital resources-are expected to become a cornerstone of the Indian education system.

The shift toward skill-based learning and vocational education is another critical trend. The evolving job market has underscored the importance of competencies beyond academic knowledge, such as critical thinking, problem-solving, communication, and teamwork. The National Education Policy (NEP) 2020 emphasizes vocational education from the secondary level, integrating practical and experiential learning into curricula. This approach aims to prepare students for diverse career pathways while aligning educational outcomes with the modern economy's demands.

Personalized learning, enabled by technological advancements, is also gaining momentum. Recognizing the diverse needs and learning styles of students, personalized learning adapts to individual strengths, weaknesses, and interests. Technologies such as adaptive learning software tailor lesson pace and content to each student's progress, while diverse educational resources address varying preferences. By ensuring equitable learning opportunities, personalized education enhances student success across backgrounds and abilities.

Holistic development, championed by the NEP 2020, represents a shift toward comprehensive education that extends beyond academics. This approach integrates physical, emotional, and social growth through curricula that include sports, arts, mindfulness, and social-emotional learning (SEL). These programs aim to foster emotional intelligence, interpersonal skills, and overall well-being, reflecting a more inclusive and supportive model of education.

These trends collectively signify a departure from traditional methods, steering Indian education toward a future that emphasizes accessibility, relevance, and comprehensive development. As these innovations continue to evolve, they will play a pivotal role in equipping students with the skills and competencies required for a rapidly changing world.

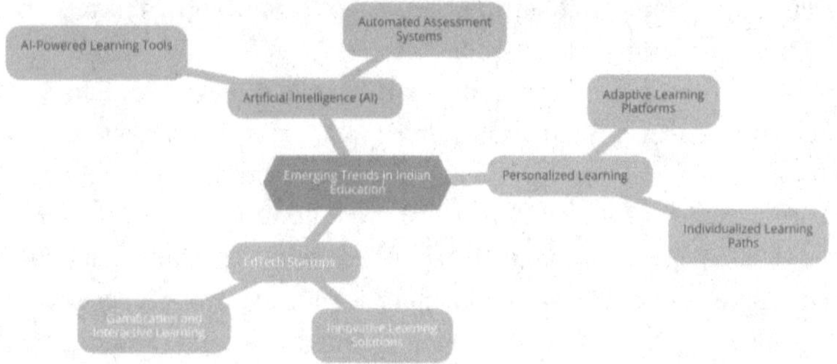

Figure 10.1: This mind map shows **Emerging Trends in Indian Education**, including:

1. **Artificial Intelligence (AI)**:
   o AI-powered learning tools and automated assessment systems.
2. **Personalized Learning**:
   o Adaptive learning platforms and individualized learning paths.
3. **EdTech Startups**:
   o Innovative learning solutions with gamification and interactive learning approaches.

Globalization is also influencing Indian education, as schools and universities seek to align their curricula with international standards. This trend is evident in the increasing popularity of international schools, the adoption of globally recognized curricula such as the International Baccalaureate (IB) and Cambridge International, and the growing emphasis on global competencies. Indian students are being encouraged to think critically about global issues, such as climate change, technology ethics, and cultural diversity, and to develop the skills needed to compete in an interconnected world. As India's economy becomes more integrated with the global market, the education system is evolving to prepare students for international opportunities.

The role of teachers is also evolving as these trends reshape education. Teachers are no longer seen as the sole source of knowledge; instead, they are becoming facilitators of learning who guide students in exploring topics, solving problems, and developing skills. Professional development for teachers is crucial in this changing landscape, as they must adapt to new teaching methods, integrate technology into the classroom, and meet the diverse needs of students. The NEP 2020 emphasizes the importance of ongoing teacher training and professional development, ensuring that educators are equipped to meet the challenges of the future.

10.2 The Role of Artificial Intelligence in Indian Classrooms

Artificial intelligence (AI) is emerging as a transformative force in education worldwide, with significant implications for Indian classrooms. By automating tasks, analyzing data, and enabling personalized learning experiences, AI offers solutions to longstanding challenges such as large class sizes, teacher shortages, and diverse student needs. Its integration into Indian education has the potential to enhance learning outcomes and increase accessibility, fostering a more equitable and engaging educational environment.

A primary impact of AI in Indian classrooms is its role in personalized learning. AI-powered platforms dynamically adapt to individual student needs by providing tailored lessons, exercises, and feedback based on real-time progress assessments. Adaptive learning systems leverage algorithms to identify each student's strengths and weaknesses, adjusting content delivery and pacing accordingly. This targeted approach allows students to receive support in mastering complex concepts while advancing in areas of proficiency. In classrooms often exceeding 40 students, AI bridges the gap in individualized attention that teachers may find challenging to provide, thereby promoting more effective learning.

AI is also reshaping assessment practices, moving beyond traditional methods such as written exams and assignments, which are often time-intensive and may not fully capture student potential. AI-driven tools, including automated essay scoring systems and intelligent tutoring platforms, offer immediate feedback, enabling students to identify and address errors as they occur. These systems facilitate continuous monitoring of student progress, allowing educators to detect patterns, predict potential learning obstacles, and implement timely interventions. By offering data-driven insights into student performance, AI supports a more nuanced and responsive approach to education.

In addition to enhancing teaching and learning processes, AI significantly alleviates the administrative burdens faced by educators. Tasks such as grading, attendance tracking, and lesson plan organization can be automated, freeing teachers to focus on direct student engagement and innovative teaching strategies. This reduction in administrative workload is particularly impactful in India, where educators often contend with extensive responsibilities, enabling them to prioritize personalized instruction and professional growth.

As AI continues to integrate into Indian classrooms, it holds the promise of addressing systemic challenges while enabling a more tailored, efficient, and student-centered educational experience. Through personalized learning, improved assessment methods, and streamlined administrative processes, AI is poised to redefine the educational landscape, fostering enhanced learning outcomes and broader access to quality education.

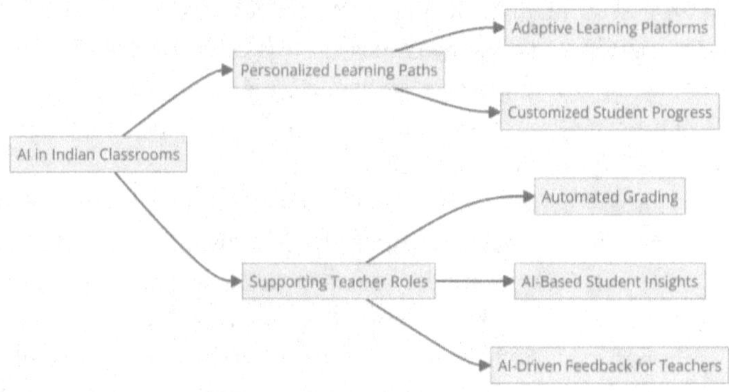

Figure 10.2: This diagram illustrates the role of **Artificial Intelligence (AI) in Indian Classrooms**:

1. **Personalized Learning Paths**:

o AI creates adaptive learning platforms and tracks customized student progress.

2. **Supporting Teacher Roles**:

Artificial intelligence (AI) is extending its impact in education by assisting teachers with automated grading, generating student insights, and providing AI-driven feedback to refine teaching strategies. AI-powered tools such as chatbots and virtual assistants are enhancing support for students beyond the classroom, offering immediate tutoring and guidance. For example, students struggling with complex mathematics problems can consult AI chatbots for step-by-step explanations. These 24/7 support systems are particularly beneficial in rural or remote areas, where access to teachers and educational resources may be limited. By bridging geographic and resource disparities, AI ensures equitable access to high-quality education, promoting continuous learning across diverse contexts.

Beyond supporting students, AI contributes to professional development for educators. AI-driven platforms analyze classroom data to provide actionable insights into teaching practices. For instance, systems can evaluate student engagement during lessons, offering feedback on effective teaching methods and identifying areas for improvement. These data-driven recommendations enable educators to refine their strategies and enhance classroom effectiveness. Additionally, AI-powered training programs provide personalized professional development, delivering resources and modules tailored to individual teachers' needs and interests. This targeted support fosters ongoing improvement in instructional quality.

The National Education Policy (NEP) 2020 underscores the importance of technology, including AI, in advancing educational outcomes in India. It advocates for the adoption of digital tools and innovative methodologies to promote equity, inclusion, and quality in education. AI is positioned as a pivotal enabler of these goals, aligning with the NEP's vision of a digitally empowered education system that supports diverse learning needs.

However, the widespread implementation of AI in Indian classrooms faces challenges, particularly related to the digital divide. Many schools, especially in rural areas, lack the technological infrastructure and internet connectivity required to fully leverage AI-driven platforms. Addressing this disparity necessitates significant investment from both government and private sectors to expand digital infrastructure and ensure equitable access. Bridging this gap is critical for enabling all students, regardless of location or socio-economic background, to benefit from AI's transformative potential in education.

10.3 Personalized Learning Paths for Indian Students

Personalized learning is gaining prominence as a transformative trend in global education, and its adoption in Indian classrooms is addressing the diverse needs of students. Unlike traditional approaches, which often employ a uniform teaching model, personalized learning focuses on tailoring education to individual needs, interests, and learning styles. In India, where classrooms frequently include students with varied abilities, experiences, and cultural backgrounds, personalized learning provides an inclusive strategy to support every learner.

Technology is integral to personalized learning, enabling the creation of customized learning paths through AI-driven platforms and adaptive learning tools. These technologies allow educators to deliver instruction that aligns with each student's pace and comprehension level. For instance, advanced learners in mathematics might be presented with more challenging problems, while those struggling with foundational concepts receive additional resources and support. This adaptive framework ensures that students engage with content appropriate to their abilities, avoiding both disengagement from overly simple tasks and frustration with overly complex material.

Student agency is another cornerstone of personalized learning, empowering learners to take control of their educational journeys. Many personalized models provide students with the flexibility to choose topics and learning methods aligned with their interests and aspirations. For example, a student interested in environmental science might explore subjects such as climate change, renewable energy, or biodiversity. This autonomy fosters deeper engagement and motivation, transforming learning into a more meaningful and enjoyable process.

In Indian classrooms, where rote memorization and standardized testing have traditionally dominated, personalized learning introduces an emphasis on critical thinking, creativity, and problem-solving. This approach is particularly effective in large, diverse classrooms, where students often progress at varying rates. Personalized platforms enable differentiated instruction, allowing teachers to meet each student's unique needs and facilitate equitable learning outcomes.

The National Education Policy (NEP) 2020 highlights the importance of personalized learning as part of its vision for a flexible and holistic educational system. Recognizing that students learn at different speeds and in diverse ways, the NEP advocates for integrating technology to create individualized learning experiences. Additionally, the policy promotes formative assessments, which provide ongoing feedback and support personalized learning objectives by tracking progress over time. These strategies align with the NEP's goal of fostering a more inclusive and adaptable education system.

Self-paced learning is a key feature of personalized education, allowing students to progress at their own speed. Traditional classrooms often impose uniform pacing, which can disadvantage both slower and faster learners. Personalized learning ensures that students grasp topics fully before advancing, creating a supportive environment conducive to mastering concepts. This flexibility is particularly valuable in Indian classrooms, where the pressures of a rigid curriculum can hinder individual learning trajectories.

Regular feedback and self-reflection are integral to personalized learning, encouraging students to monitor their progress and refine their strategies. Digital platforms provide real-time feedback on assignments, quizzes, and projects, enabling students to identify areas for improvement and celebrate milestones. This continuous feedback loop promotes a growth mindset, reframing education as an iterative process rather than a series of high-stakes evaluations. In India, where traditional assessments often focus on final examinations, personalized learning offers a comprehensive alternative that emphasizes individual growth and development.

Personalized learning also extends beyond school hours, with online courses, educational apps, and virtual tutoring providing opportunities for flexible, self-directed learning. This accessibility is particularly impactful in India, where students in rural areas or with long commutes face barriers to traditional education. By bridging the gap between urban and rural resources, personalized learning ensures equitable access to quality education.

10.4 Preparing Indian Educators for Future Challenges

As India's education landscape evolves, equipping educators to navigate future challenges is increasingly vital. The role of teachers is transitioning from traditional knowledge dissemination to facilitating learning, necessitating the adoption of innovative teaching methods, the integration of technology, and responsiveness to diverse student needs. Ensuring that teachers are prepared for these changes requires targeted professional development and access to tools that enable success in a dynamic educational environment.

Professional development is central to preparing educators for the demands of modern education. Continuous learning and upskilling enable teachers to stay abreast of advancements in educational technology, pedagogical strategies, and national policies such as the NEP 2020. Schools and institutions play a critical role by offering workshops, seminars, and online courses that equip educators with relevant skills and knowledge. For example, training focused on integrating digital tools into classrooms or implementing personalized learning models empowers teachers to adopt innovative practices that enhance teaching efficacy and student engagement.

Integrating technology into teaching is a key focus of educator preparation, as digital learning tools become increasingly prevalent in classrooms. Teachers must develop proficiency in leveraging technology to improve engagement and outcomes. From smartboards and educational applications to AI-powered platforms, digital tools are reshaping instructional practices. Professional development programs emphasizing digital literacy and instructional technology are essential for ensuring that educators can create interactive, student-centered learning environments. For instance, training on digital assessment tools enables teachers to provide real-time feedback, while tutorials on online collaboration platforms help facilitate group projects, fostering skills critical for both academic and professional success.

As technology continues to transform education, providing educators with ongoing support and resources will remain integral to preparing them for the future. By aligning professional development with emerging trends and equipping teachers with practical strategies, Indian schools can ensure that educators are well-prepared to lead classrooms that inspire and empower the next generation.

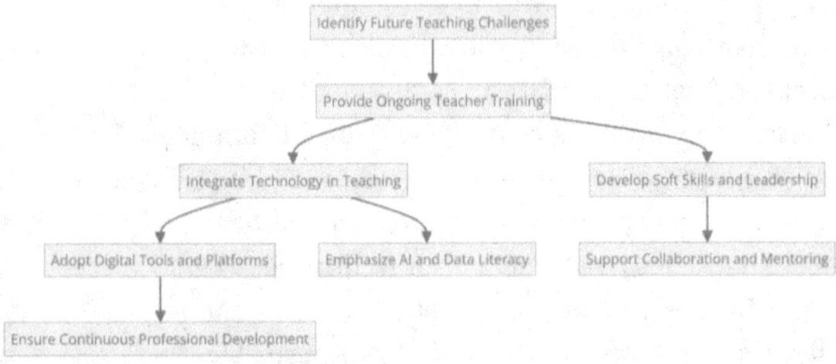

Figure 10.3: This flowchart outlines the steps for **Preparing Indian Educators for Future Challenges**, with a focus on training and technology adoption:

1. **Identify Future Teaching Challenges**:
o Recognize the evolving challenges in education that teachers will face.
2. **Provide Ongoing Teacher Training**:
o Ensure continuous training programs for educators to stay updated.
3. **Integrate Technology in Teaching**:
o Encourage the use of digital tools and platforms.
o **Adopt Digital Tools and Platforms**: Emphasize the use of technology in classrooms.
o **Emphasize AI and Data Literacy**: Teachers need to be familiar with AI and data-driven teaching.
4. **Develop Soft Skills and Leadership**:
o Build leadership and collaboration skills among educators.
o **Support Collaboration and Mentoring**: Foster a collaborative environment where teachers mentor one another.

5. **Ensure Continuous Professional Development**:
   o Maintain ongoing development to keep teachers equipped for the future.

The transformation of India's education system is contingent on equipping educators with the skills and strategies needed to navigate an evolving pedagogical landscape. Teachers are transitioning from traditional roles as knowledge dispensers to facilitators of student-centered learning, necessitating the adoption of new teaching methodologies, technological integration, and inclusive practices. Addressing these needs requires robust professional development, systemic support, and a culture of continuous improvement.

The shift toward student-centered learning is driving the adoption of active pedagogical approaches such as inquiry-based learning, problem-solving, and experiential education. These methods encourage critical thinking, creativity, and collaboration, moving beyond rote memorization and lecture-based instruction. Teachers must be trained to design lessons that allow students to explore real-world issues, engage in hands-on activities, and collaborate with peers. Such strategies prepare students for the complexities of modern life while fostering deeper engagement and understanding.

Meeting the diverse needs of India's student population requires inclusive education practices. Classrooms encompass learners from varied socio-economic backgrounds, cultural communities, and abilities. Teachers must be equipped to employ differentiated instruction, adapt lessons to accommodate diverse learning styles, and cultivate inclusive classroom environments. Professional development in inclusive practices ensures that all students, regardless of their circumstances, have access to equitable and high-quality education.

Social and emotional learning (SEL) is another critical area for educator preparation. Highlighted in the NEP 2020, SEL emphasizes the holistic development of students, including emotional intelligence, resilience, and interpersonal skills. Teachers play a pivotal role in fostering a classroom culture that supports these attributes, helping students manage challenges and build healthy relationships. Training programs focused on SEL equip teachers with strategies to integrate these skills into the curriculum, enhancing students' overall well-being and academic success.

Collaboration among educators is vital for navigating the challenges of modern teaching. Professional learning communities provide a platform for teachers to exchange ideas, share best practices, and innovate collaboratively. Through such networks, educators can design interdisciplinary projects, incorporate digital tools into their pedagogy, and refine their approaches based on peer feedback. These collaborative efforts ensure adaptability and foster a culture of continuous improvement.

Leadership development is essential to creating environments conducive to educational innovation. School leaders must be equipped to guide systemic change, support teachers, and promote a vision of excellence. Programs that enhance leadership capabilities in areas such as change management, school culture, and strategic planning empower administrators to drive meaningful improvements in teaching and learning practices.

A growth mindset among educators is key to embracing the dynamic nature of education. Teachers must remain open to experimenting with new approaches, reflecting on their practices, and committing to lifelong learning. Schools can support this by encouraging reflective practices, fostering professional curiosity, and promoting resilience in the face of evolving demands.

Government initiatives play a central role in driving educational reform. The NEP 2020 provides a framework for reimagining education, emphasizing multidisciplinary learning, vocational training, technology integration, and foundational skills. Programs such as the Digital India initiative, Samagra Shiksha Abhiyan, and DIKSHA platform address gaps in access and resources, particularly in underserved areas. Efforts to improve teacher quality, such as the NISHTHA initiative, focus on upskilling educators in modern methodologies and digital literacy.

Incorporating vocational education into the curriculum aligns with the NEP's emphasis on practical skills and employability. Initiatives such as the Pradhan Mantri Kaushal Vikas Yojana (PMKVY) and partnerships with industry stakeholders ensure that students are equipped with market-relevant competencies. Additionally, programs promoting equity, such as the Right to Education Act and targeted scholarships, work to bridge socio-economic divides.

10.6 EdTech Startups Transforming Indian Classrooms

India's education technology (EdTech) sector is experiencing rapid growth, fundamentally transforming traditional learning environments. Leveraging advancements in digital tools and online platforms, EdTech startups are reshaping education by making it more accessible, personalized, and engaging. In a country where challenges such as large class sizes, unequal resource distribution, and an emphasis on rote learning persist, these innovations offer effective solutions to bridge gaps and enhance the educational experience for students nationwide.

A primary contribution of EdTech startups is the democratization of education. Platforms like Byju's, Unacademy, and Vedantu provide high-quality learning materials, accessible to students irrespective of their geographic or socio-economic backgrounds. These digital platforms enable learners in remote areas to access resources such as video lessons, quizzes, and interactive exercises, effectively narrowing the urban-rural education divide. For instance, a student from a village with limited schooling opportunities can engage with expert-curated content via mobile applications, bringing top-tier educational tools directly to their fingertips.

Personalized learning, a hallmark of modern education, has been significantly advanced by EdTech. Adaptive learning platforms powered by artificial intelligence (AI) assess students' progress and tailor content to their individual needs. Startups like Toppr and Embibe offer customized pathways, adjusting difficulty levels and recommending targeted practice areas. This approach ensures that students receive support where they struggle while advancing more quickly in areas of strength, fostering both comprehension and confidence.

Interactive learning methods, facilitated by EdTech platforms, are transforming passive educational models into dynamic, student-centered experiences. Platforms such as Vedantu and WhiteHat Jr. offer live, interactive classes where students can engage with teachers and peers in real time, fostering deeper engagement and collaborative learning. Gamification tools like Quizizz and Kahoot! integrate competitive quizzes and rewards, making learning enjoyable and memorable. This shift from passive reception to active participation enhances retention and promotes a deeper understanding of material.

Teachers also benefit from the tools developed by EdTech startups, which streamline classroom management and professional growth. Platforms like Teachmint and Classplus provide resources for lesson planning, assessments, and communication with parents. Additionally, these tools offer professional development opportunities, enabling teachers to refine their methodologies, collaborate with peers, and stay updated on emerging trends. By equipping educators with digital tools, EdTech enhances teaching practices and improves student outcomes.

The integration of EdTech in Indian classrooms has significantly improved assessment practices. Traditional exams often provide limited insights into a student's learning journey, whereas digital platforms enable continuous monitoring and formative assessments. Tools like Google Classroom and Microsoft Teams allow teachers to track assignments and participation in real time, offering immediate feedback and addressing learning gaps as they arise. This real-time evaluation supports individualized instruction and ensures students remain on track.

The rise of coding and STEM education is another significant development led by EdTech startups. Companies such as WhiteHat Jr., CampK12, and Coding Ninjas offer courses in programming, app development, robotics, and other technical skills. These initiatives equip students with competencies essential for the future workforce, fostering problem-solving, creativity, and innovation. By introducing hands-on, project-based learning, these platforms inspire students to develop technical expertise and adapt to rapidly evolving industries.

EdTech platforms also address exam preparation, a central concern for Indian students. Startups like Unacademy, Gradeup, and Testbook provide tailored resources for competitive exams such as IIT-JEE, NEET, and UPSC. With flexible learning options, these platforms allow students to access expert guidance, video lectures, mock tests, and study plans, ensuring comprehensive preparation irrespective of location.

Government support has been instrumental in fostering EdTech growth in India. Initiatives such as Digital India and partnerships between EdTech companies and public institutions have expanded access to digital learning tools. The National Education Policy (NEP) 2020 emphasizes integrating technology into teaching processes, encouraging schools to adopt innovative tools that enhance educational outcomes. By creating a conducive ecosystem, the government is laying a foundation for a technology-driven education system.

10.7 Global Comparisons: Indian Education and the World

India's education system is undergoing significant reform, prompting comparisons with global counterparts in terms of structure, pedagogy, and outcomes. These comparisons offer valuable insights into India's strengths and areas for improvement while highlighting challenges and opportunities as the country strives to align with international standards without losing its cultural and social uniqueness.

A key difference lies in the emphasis on rote learning versus critical thinking and problem-solving. In many Western nations, such as Finland, Canada, and the United States, education prioritizes creativity, independent thought, and practical applications of knowledge. These systems encourage inquiry, hands-on learning, and real-world problem-solving, fostering deeper engagement and conceptual understanding. Conversely, the Indian system has traditionally relied on rote memorization, largely driven by the demands of standardized exams. The

National Education Policy (NEP) 2020 seeks to address this by promoting experiential and skill-based learning, steering Indian education toward approaches seen in global leaders like Finland and Singapore. By incorporating inquiry-based projects and reducing reliance on high-stakes testing, the NEP aims to nurture critical thinking, flexibility, and creativity.

The structure and accessibility of education systems also reveal important contrasts. Countries such as Germany and Switzerland are noted for their robust vocational training frameworks, offering students multiple pathways, including apprenticeships and industry-linked programs. These systems ensure that students pursuing non-academic careers receive quality training and opportunities. Similarly, NEP 2020 emphasizes integrating vocational education into Indian curricula from an early stage, inspired by models like Germany's dual education system, which balances theoretical knowledge with practical industry experience.

Equity and access present a significant challenge for Indian education in comparison to global benchmarks. Countries like Finland, Norway, and Canada prioritize equitable public education, investing heavily to minimize socio-economic disparities. These nations ensure high-quality teachers, resources, and infrastructure for all students, regardless of background. India, however, faces stark inequalities, particularly between urban and rural schools and between government and private institutions. While elite private schools deliver world-class education, a majority of students in rural and underserved areas lack basic facilities, trained educators, and digital tools. Initiatives such as Samagra Shiksha Abhiyan and Digital India aim to reduce these disparities by improving infrastructure and expanding access to digital resources. However, achieving equity on par with global leaders remains a formidable challenge.

Teacher training and professional development are areas where international systems provide valuable lessons. In countries such as Singapore, South Korea, and Japan, teachers undergo rigorous training and continuous professional development throughout their careers. Seen as respected professionals, they receive mentorship and support to maintain high teaching standards. The NEP 2020 acknowledges the need for improving teacher education in India, advocating for ongoing learning, mentorship, and exposure to innovative teaching methodologies. Strengthening teacher quality is essential for creating dynamic, student-centered learning environments and aligning India's education standards with those of high-performing nations.

Technology integration is another domain of comparison. Countries like South

Korea, Estonia, and Finland lead in incorporating digital tools into education, leveraging AI, personalized platforms, and technology-driven assessments. India is advancing in this area through EdTech startups and government-backed digital learning initiatives. However, the digital divide remains a significant obstacle, particularly in rural regions where access to infrastructure is limited. Estonia's comprehensive nationwide digital education initiatives provide a model for India to emulate as it scales up its digital capacity.

In higher education, global rankings highlight gaps between Indian and international institutions. Universities in the United States, the United Kingdom, and other Western countries consistently dominate rankings, with only a few Indian institutions, such as the IITs and IIMs, achieving global recognition. Broader challenges, including limited funding, low research output, and insufficient international collaboration, hinder India's higher education sector. Addressing these issues requires investment in research infrastructure, efforts to attract global talent, and fostering a culture of innovation to position Indian universities as competitive on the world stage.

10.8 Final Thoughts and the Road Ahead for Education in India

As India moves into a transformative phase of its education system, the implementation of the National Education Policy (NEP) 2020 represents a crucial milestone in modernizing and reimagining how education is delivered. By emphasizing technology integration, skill-based learning, holistic development, and inclusivity, the NEP signals a shift from traditional models centered on rote learning and examinations. This transition requires sustained innovation and commitment to ensure equitable access to quality education for all students, equipping them to excel in an increasingly complex and interconnected world.

The NEP's focus on experiential learning, inquiry-based approaches, and problem-solving underscores the move toward a student-centered education system. This shift aligns with global trends prioritizing critical thinking, creativity, and adaptability-skills essential for navigating a rapidly changing landscape. Historically characterized by a strong foundation in memorization and theoretical knowledge, Indian education is evolving to include opportunities for hands-on learning, peer collaboration, and real-world problem-solving. Such approaches not only enhance academic outcomes but also foster personal growth, emotional intelligence, and social adaptability, preparing students to thrive in diverse and dynamic environments.

Technology will be pivotal in shaping the future of Indian education. The rapid expansion of EdTech startups, AI-driven tools, and online learning platforms is already broadening access to quality education across the nation. With improvements in digital infrastructure, particularly in rural areas, technology can bridge long-standing gaps, providing students with access to resources previously beyond their reach. The NEP's emphasis on digital literacy and the integration of technology into classrooms is driving this transformation, equipping students with the digital skills essential for success in the modern workforce.

Teacher development will play a foundational role in ensuring the success of these reforms. As the role of educators evolves from disseminators of knowledge to facilitators of learning, continuous professional development will be critical. Training in new pedagogical approaches, digital literacy, and inclusive teaching practices will empower teachers to meet the diverse needs of their students. The NEP's emphasis on mentorship and ongoing professional development aims to create a dynamic and adaptable teaching workforce capable of guiding students through the complexities of contemporary education.

Equity in education remains a critical issue to address as India modernizes its education system. Despite progress, disparities in access persist between urban and rural areas and across socio-economic groups. Programs like Samagra Shiksha Abhiyan and Digital India have made notable contributions to reducing these gaps, yet additional efforts are needed. Investment in infrastructure, targeted financial aid for disadvantaged students, and ensuring the presence of well-trained educators in all schools will be essential for achieving equitable outcomes.

The NEP's focus on vocational education represents a significant step in aligning education with industry needs. By integrating vocational training into school curricula from an early stage, the policy aims to equip students with practical, industry-relevant skills alongside academic knowledge. This dual approach will expand career opportunities for students while addressing the growing skills gap in the workforce. As industries undergo rapid technological advancements and automation, this initiative ensures that students are prepared for the evolving demands of the economy, fostering both individual success and broader economic growth.

India's education system is at a pivotal moment of transformation, guided by the NEP's vision of an inclusive, skill-oriented, and technologically integrated future.

CHAPTER 11

IMPACT OF NEP 2020 ON TEACHING METHODS IN INDIA

11.1 Overview of NEP 2020: Key Reforms and Objectives

The National Education Policy (NEP) 2020 marks a pivotal reform in India's education system, replacing the 1986 framework to address the evolving needs of students in the 21st century. By emphasizing critical thinking, creativity, and holistic development, the policy aims to modernize education and equip students with the skills required to navigate a rapidly transforming global landscape.

A cornerstone of the NEP 2020 is the transition from rote memorization to an experiential, skill-based approach. By reducing curriculum content to core concepts, the policy prioritizes critical thinking, conceptual understanding, and problem-solving. This reorientation seeks to cultivate independent thought and encourage the application of knowledge to real-world challenges. By moving away from a high-pressure, exam-centric system, the policy envisions a more engaging and dynamic educational environment.

Inclusivity and equitable access to education are central to the NEP 2020's objectives. A significant reform under the policy is the universalization of early childhood care and education (ECCE), ensuring that all children have access to quality preschool education from the age of three. Recognizing the foundational role of early education in cognitive, emotional, and social development, the policy integrates ECCE into the broader school framework to address disparities from the earliest stages of education.

The policy further emphasizes holistic and multidisciplinary learning by encouraging students to engage with diverse fields, including arts, sciences, humanities, and vocational education. This shift aims to break away from rigid academic streams, fostering a well-rounded education that equips students with a broad skill set and the flexibility to adapt to a dynamic global workforce. By integrating varied disciplines, the NEP promotes not only academic achievement but also personal and social growth.

Technology and digital learning are integral components of the NEP 2020, reflecting the increasing importance of digital tools in education. The policy advocates for the incorporation of online platforms, educational applications, and digital assessments to enhance accessibility and quality, particularly in underserved regions. By leveraging technology, the NEP envisions inclusive and equitable learning environments where all students, regardless of socio-economic background, have access to high-quality resources and opportunities.

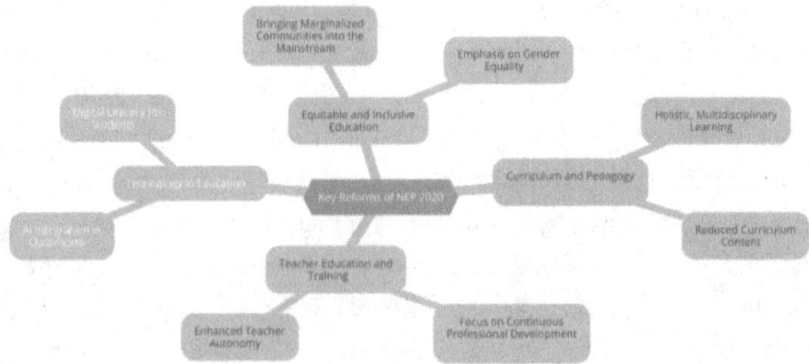

Figure 11.1: This mind map illustrates the **Key Reforms of NEP 2020** and their impact on Indian education:

1. **Curriculum and Pedagogy**:

o Promotes holistic, multidisciplinary learning with a reduced curriculum load.

2. **Teacher Education and Training**:

o Focuses on continuous professional development and increased teacher autonomy.

3. **Technology in Education**:

o Integrates AI in classrooms and emphasizes digital literacy.

4. **Equitable and Inclusive Education**:

o Aims to bring marginalized communities into mainstream education and emphasizes gender equality.

The policy also emphasizes the importance of teacher training and professional development. Recognizing that teachers are the cornerstone of any education system, NEP 2020 calls for continuous professional development programs to ensure that educators are equipped with the latest pedagogical tools and methodologies. The policy advocates for the use of digital platforms to provide ongoing training and support for teachers, enabling them to stay updated with new teaching practices and effectively implement the changes outlined in the NEP. In terms of assessment, NEP 2020 seeks to move away from high-stakes, summative exams and toward a more holistic evaluation system. The policy promotes the use of formative assessments, which provide ongoing feedback to students and help identify areas for improvement. Additionally, NEP 2020 calls for competency-based assessments that focus on students' understanding of key concepts and their ability to apply their knowledge in practical situations. This shift in assessment practices is intended to reduce the stress associated with exams and promote a deeper understanding of the subject matter.

11.2 Shifts in Pedagogical Approaches Under NEP 2020

The National Education Policy (NEP) 2020 has introduced a transformative shift in India's education system, prioritizing interactive, student-centered pedagogies over traditional methods rooted in rote memorization and passive instruction. By fostering critical thinking, creativity, and practical knowledge application, the NEP envisions a dynamic educational framework designed to equip students with the competencies required for success in the 21st century.

A central reform introduced by the NEP 2020 is the emphasis on experiential and inquiry-based learning. This pedagogical shift encourages students to actively engage with their subjects through exploration and hands-on activities, rather than merely memorizing information. For instance, science education may involve experiments and fieldwork, while social studies could incorporate project-based investigations into topics like climate change or urban development. Such approaches enhance engagement and promote the development of problem-solving, collaboration, and communication skills.

The NEP also advocates for interdisciplinary learning, breaking down traditional academic silos to offer a more integrated and holistic educational experience. By linking subjects such as environmental science with economics, geography, and ethics, the policy fosters a comprehensive understanding of complex issues. This multidisciplinary framework aligns with the NEP's goal of holistic development, equipping students to critically analyze real-world challenges and devise innovative solutions.

A key aspect of the pedagogical reforms is the emphasis on cultivating higher-order thinking skills. Moving beyond lecture-based teaching, the NEP encourages methods such as group discussions, debates, and problem-solving exercises to promote active engagement and deep learning. These strategies help students analyze, evaluate, and synthesize information, developing critical thinking capabilities essential for academic and professional success (Figure 11.2).

Personalized learning forms another cornerstone of the NEP's reforms. Recognizing that students have diverse learning styles and paces, the policy advocates for adaptive teaching methods that cater to individual needs. Technologies that adjust lesson content and pacing based on a student's progress are central to this approach. For example, while advanced learners can explore more challenging material, those requiring additional support receive tailored resources. This adaptive framework ensures equitable learning opportunities, enabling all students to progress effectively at their own pace.

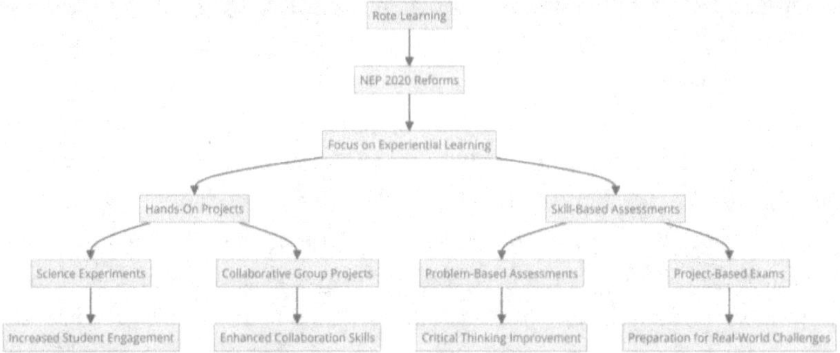

Figure 11.2: This flowchart illustrates the **Shift from Rote Learning to Experiential and Skills-Based Learning** under NEP 2020:

1. **Rote Learning**:
   o Previously emphasized in the traditional education system.
2. **NEP 2020 Reforms**:
   o Aimed to shift focus to **Experiential Learning**.
3. **Hands-On Projects**:
   o Includes **Science Experiments** and **Collaborative Group Projects** to actively engage students.
4. **Skill-Based Assessments**:
   o Uses **Problem-Based Assessments** and **Project-Based Exams** to evaluate real-world skills.
5. **Outcomes**:
   o **Increased Student Engagement**: Hands-on projects keep students more involved.
   o **Enhanced Collaboration Skills**: Group projects foster teamwork.
   o **Critical Thinking Improvement**: Skill-based assessments develop critical thinking.
   o **Preparation for Real-World Challenges**: Project-based exams prepare students for real-life scenarios.

The integration of technology into teaching and learning is also a central component of the pedagogical shift under NEP 2020. Digital tools such as online learning platforms, interactive apps, and AI-driven assessments are being used to enhance the classroom experience and provide students with more personalized and interactive learning opportunities. Teachers are encouraged to incorporate digital resources into their lessons, enabling students to engage with content in new and innovative ways. For instance, virtual labs can allow students to conduct experiments online, while AI-powered platforms can provide real-time feedback on assignments and assessments. The use of technology not only makes learning more accessible but also helps prepare students for a future where digital literacy is increasingly important. The NEP's focus on collaborative learning is another significant departure from traditional teaching methods. The policy encourages teachers to create opportunities for students to work together on group projects and activities, helping them develop teamwork and communication skills. Collaborative learning not only fosters a sense of community in the classroom but also allows students to learn from each other's perspectives and experiences. This approach is particularly important in today's globalized world, where the ability to work effectively in teams is a crucial skill.

Assessment practices are also undergoing a transformation under NEP 2020. Traditional high-stakes exams, which often encourage rote memorization, are being replaced by more formative and competency-based assessments. These new assessment methods focus on evaluating students' understanding of key concepts and their ability to apply knowledge in real-world situations. For example, instead of a written exam, students might be assessed through a project or presentation that requires them to demonstrate their learning in a practical context. This shift in assessment aligns with the broader goal of promoting deeper learning and reducing the emphasis on exams as the sole measure of success.

11.3 Integration of Multidisciplinary and Holistic Education

The National Education Policy (NEP) 2020 introduces a paradigm shift in Indian education, emphasizing multidisciplinary and holistic learning. Moving beyond traditional, compartmentalized subject-specific instruction, the policy fosters an integrated approach that encourages students to explore diverse fields of study. By promoting flexibility, inclusivity, and the integration of academics with vocational and extracurricular activities, NEP 2020 aims to support the intellectual, emotional, social, and physical development of students.

The multidisciplinary framework of NEP 2020 dismantles rigid subject boundaries, enabling students to engage with a broad array of disciplines. For instance, studying environmental science may involve examining intersections with economics, history, and geography to understand the broader implications of environmental issues on policies, historical contexts, and societal dynamics. This interconnected approach equips students with critical and creative thinking skills necessary to address complex global challenges.

Historically, Indian students have been required to choose narrow academic streams, such as science, commerce, or arts, at an early stage, limiting exposure to other fields. NEP 2020 seeks to eliminate these constraints, allowing students to combine subjects from different streams to align their education with personal interests and career goals. For example, a student with interests in both biology and literature might explore science communication or medical humanities, fields that reflect the increasing value of interdisciplinary expertise in a dynamic job market.

Holistic education under NEP 2020 extends beyond academic learning to include physical education, arts, music, and life skills, emphasizing the importance of fostering a well-rounded personality. Schools are encouraged to incorporate arts and sports into the curriculum, promoting creativity, teamwork, and resilience. Activities such as art projects, music performances, and sports competitions provide students with opportunities to balance intellectual development with physical and emotional well-being.

Experiential and skills-based learning is central to NEP 2020's vision. The policy moves away from a sole reliance on theoretical instruction, advocating for practical applications of knowledge through real-world experiences. Vocational education is integral to this shift, offering students opportunities to gain skills in areas such as coding, carpentry, agriculture, and entrepreneurship. By embedding vocational training within the academic framework, the NEP prepares students to excel both academically and professionally, ensuring alignment with workforce demands.

Life skills are another critical focus of the policy, with an emphasis on emotional intelligence, communication, and resilience. Social-emotional learning (SEL) is highlighted, encouraging schools to teach students how to manage emotions, build relationships, and make informed decisions. These skills are crucial for navigating personal and professional challenges, fostering effective collaboration, and resolving conflicts in diverse contexts.

NEP 2020 also prioritizes environmental education and sustainability, urging schools to integrate topics such as climate change, biodiversity, and conservation into the curriculum. By engaging in local projects, such as waste reduction or water conservation initiatives, students develop practical problem-solving and collaboration skills while gaining a deeper understanding of environmental issues.

The inclusion of health and well-being in the curriculum reflects the policy's commitment to holistic development. Topics such as nutrition, mental health, and physical fitness are integrated to promote healthy lifestyles. Schools are encouraged to provide opportunities for physical activity, mindfulness, and open discussions on mental health, ensuring that students' physical and mental well-being are supported alongside academic growth.

This multidisciplinary and holistic vision aligns with global education trends seen in countries such as Finland, Singapore, and Canada, where integrated curricula and whole-child development are prioritized. NEP 2020 mirrors these models, preparing Indian students to become adaptable, creative, and lifelong learners in an interconnected and rapidly evolving world. By fostering diverse interests and equipping students with a broad range of skills, the policy ensures they are well-prepared to thrive in the complexities of the modern global landscape.

11.4 Promoting Experiential and Skills-Based Learning

The National Education Policy (NEP) 2020 introduces a transformative framework for education in India, emphasizing experiential and skills-based learning to move beyond traditional rote methods. This approach prioritizes the application of knowledge in real-world contexts, fostering practical skills and adaptability to equip students for the complexities of a rapidly changing global environment.

Experiential learning, as outlined in the policy, encourages students to engage actively with their education through hands-on activities, projects, and fieldwork. Rather than relying on rote memorization of theoretical concepts, students participate in tasks that connect academic content to real-world challenges. For instance, in environmental science, students might engage in community initiatives focused on waste reduction or water conservation, integrating classroom knowledge with practical applications to address pressing societal issues.

Project-based learning is a central feature of this paradigm, with NEP 2020 advocating for students to tackle real-life problems collaboratively. This method involves investigating issues such as local traffic congestion or environmental degradation through data collection, analysis, and solution development. Such projects cultivate critical thinking, communication, teamwork, and leadership skills while deepening subject knowledge. The emphasis on these competencies aligns education with the demands of a technology-driven, fast-paced world, ensuring students are prepared to adapt and innovate in diverse contexts.

Vocational education plays an integral role in the policy's vision for inclusive and practical learning. Starting from Grade 6, students are introduced to vocational subjects, including carpentry, coding, agriculture, and entrepreneurship. By integrating these skills into the mainstream curriculum, NEP 2020 eliminates the divide between academic and vocational tracks, enabling students to explore diverse career pathways while acquiring practical expertise alongside theoretical knowledge.

The policy also underscores the importance of life skills and social-emotional learning (SEL). Skills such as decision-making, conflict resolution, and time management are incorporated into the curriculum to enhance students' personal and professional capabilities. SEL fosters emotional intelligence, empathy, and relationship management, equipping students to navigate challenges with resilience and maintain effective interpersonal interactions, both in the workplace and in daily life.

A notable advantage of experiential and skills-based education is its capacity to deeply engage students. Traditional systems, often focused on memorization and examinations, risk disengagement by disconnecting learning from practical relevance. Experiential methods, by involving active participation and real-world problem-solving, promote student ownership of learning and a more profound understanding of academic material.

The integration of digital literacy and technology is another critical component of NEP 2020. Recognizing the central role of technology in the modern economy, the policy emphasizes developing students' digital competencies through tools such as coding programs, online research platforms, and digital collaboration technologies. For example, students might participate in app development or website creation, simultaneously enhancing their technical skills and fostering creativity and innovation.

Teachers are pivotal to the successful implementation of this shift toward experiential and skills-based learning. Their role transitions from traditional lecturers to facilitators who guide and support students in active learning processes. To ensure effective delivery, professional development programs focusing on experiential methods and technology integration are essential. By equipping teachers with the necessary skills and resources, NEP 2020 aims to cultivate interactive and dynamic learning environments that blend academic rigor with practical relevance.

11.5 NEP's Emphasis on Technology and Digital Learning

The National Education Policy (NEP) 2020 underscores the transformative role of technology and digital learning in reshaping India's educational landscape. Recognizing the pervasive influence of digital tools in modern education, the policy provides a comprehensive framework to integrate technology into teaching and learning, with a focus on inclusivity, accessibility, and alignment with the demands of a digital era. This vision aims to prepare students and educators for a technology-driven future while addressing long-standing challenges in equitable access to quality education.

A key component of NEP 2020 is the promotion of online and blended learning models. Lessons from the COVID-19 pandemic have reinforced the necessity of digital platforms in ensuring educational continuity. Blended learning, which combines traditional classroom methods with online resources, enhances flexibility and personalization in education. Students can access materials at their own pace, revisiting challenging concepts as needed. For instance, a student grappling with complex mathematical principles can utilize online tutorials and exercises to strengthen comprehension, complementing classroom instruction.

The establishment of virtual platforms and centralized educational repositories is another significant initiative under NEP 2020. The proposed National Educational Technology Forum (NETF) aims to facilitate dialogue and innovation in the integration of technology within education. By identifying best practices, sharing digital resources, and supporting educators and institutions, the NETF seeks to bridge the gap between technology and pedagogy. Additionally, the creation of online libraries and content databases will provide high-quality, easily accessible materials to students nationwide, particularly in rural and underserved regions.

Digital literacy forms a cornerstone of the policy's approach, recognizing its essential role in the modern workforce. NEP 2020 advocates for the introduction of digital literacy programs at early education levels, equipping students with the skills to navigate digital platforms, utilize software tools, and comprehend foundational concepts such as cybersecurity and data privacy. By embedding these competencies early, the policy ensures that students are prepared to engage with an increasingly technology-centric world.

The adoption of advanced technologies, including artificial intelligence (AI) and virtual reality (VR), is also emphasized in NEP 2020. AI-powered platforms offer personalized learning experiences by adapting content to individual student needs, identifying learning gaps, and providing tailored interventions. VR enhances traditional education by enabling immersive experiences, such as virtual explorations of historical events or scientific phenomena, fostering deeper engagement and understanding.

For educators, the policy highlights the critical need for professional development in educational technology. As digital tools become integral to classrooms, teachers must be equipped to effectively incorporate these innovations into their pedagogy. NEP 2020 supports online training modules and workshops focused on digital pedagogy, ensuring that educators can skillfully manage both remote and hybrid classrooms while maintaining student engagement and learning outcomes.

Technology also enhances inclusivity in education, addressing the needs of students with disabilities and those in remote regions. Assistive technologies, such as screen readers, voice recognition software, and interactive applications, provide greater accessibility for students with diverse abilities. Online learning platforms further bridge geographical divides, granting students in rural areas access to quality resources and instruction often limited to urban centers. These measures align with the policy's broader goal of reducing inequities in educational opportunities.

Digital tools also enable a shift in assessment practices, moving away from traditional exams toward formative, competency-based evaluations. Online assessments provide immediate feedback, facilitating continuous learning and allowing teachers to monitor student progress in real time. Tailored assessments adapt to individual student capabilities, offering personalized challenges and promoting a more nuanced understanding of learning outcomes.

11.6 Impact of NEP 2020 on Teacher Training and Professional Development

The National Education Policy (NEP) 2020 places a strong emphasis on the professional development and training of teachers, recognizing them as the cornerstone of a quality education system. The policy acknowledges that teachers must be well-equipped with the skills, knowledge, and resources necessary to meet the evolving demands of modern education. NEP 2020 introduces comprehensive reforms aimed at improving the quality of teacher education, providing continuous professional development, and ensuring that teachers are empowered to play a central role in transforming the education system. One of the most significant impacts of NEP 2020 on teacher training is the shift toward continuous professional development (CPD). In the past, teacher training often consisted of one-time certification programs with little emphasis on ongoing development. NEP 2020 recognizes that education is a dynamic field and that teachers must continually update their skills to keep pace with new teaching methodologies, technological advancements, and the changing needs of students. The policy recommends the establishment of a dedicated platform for

CPD, where teachers can access online courses, workshops, and training programs throughout their careers. This approach ensures that teachers remain lifelong learners, constantly enhancing their skills and staying informed about best practices in education **(Figure 11.3)**.

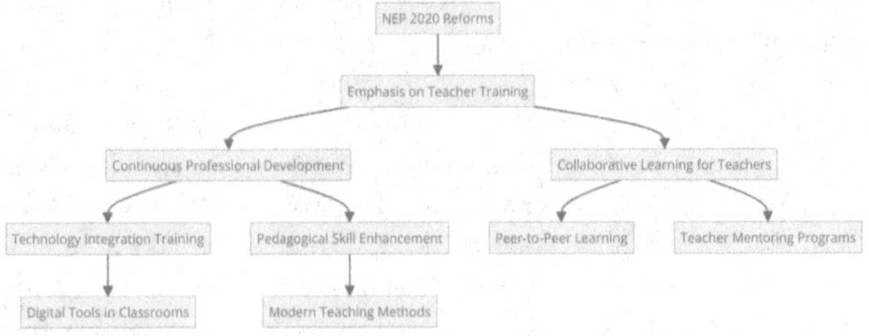

Figure 11.3: This diagram highlights the **Emphasis on Teacher Training** under NEP 2020:

1. **Continuous Professional Development**:
   o Ongoing training focusing on modern teaching approaches.
2. **Technology Integration Training**:
   o Teachers are trained to incorporate digital tools into classrooms.
3. **Pedagogical Skill Enhancement**:
   o Emphasis on improving teaching skills for more effective learning outcomes.
4. **Collaborative Learning for Teachers**:

The National Education Policy (NEP) 2020 introduces a transformative framework for teacher professional development in India, emphasizing continuous learning, collaboration, and innovation to enhance teaching practices nationwide. Recognizing teachers as the cornerstone of quality education, the policy advocates a multifaceted approach to equip educators with the skills and knowledge required to meet the evolving demands of modern classrooms.

A key focus of the policy is on subject-specific training in addition to general pedagogical enhancement. NEP 2020 underscores the importance of deepening content knowledge to enable teachers to effectively communicate complex concepts. For instance, science educators may participate in workshops on advancements in physics or chemistry, while language teachers explore innovative methods for teaching grammar and reading comprehension. This targeted training ensures that teachers are not only adept at instructional strategies but also have a firm grasp of their subject matter.

The integration of technology into professional development is another cornerstone of the policy. With digital tools becoming integral to education, NEP 2020 emphasizes training teachers to use educational technologies effectively. Digital literacy programs, integrated into teacher education, aim to familiarize educators with online teaching platforms, interactive lesson design, and AI-driven tools. For example, teachers might learn to create engaging online lessons, utilize digital assessments for real-time feedback, or incorporate virtual reality to provide immersive learning experiences. These skills are essential for fostering a tech-savvy and adaptable teaching workforce.

Flexibility in professional development pathways is also a critical component of NEP 2020. By expanding access to online and distance learning programs, the policy ensures that teachers in rural or underserved areas can participate in training without logistical barriers. These programs allow educators to pursue certification and upskilling at their convenience, accommodating diverse schedules and personal circumstances. This inclusive approach democratizes access to professional development, bridging geographic and socio-economic gaps.

The policy further promotes collaboration through Professional Learning Communities (PLCs), where teachers can exchange ideas, share resources, and collectively innovate. These communities encourage interdisciplinary collaboration and peer learning, fostering a supportive environment for professional growth. For example, teachers might co-develop projects that integrate science and social studies or collaborate on strategies for differentiated instruction. By facilitating continuous interaction among educators, PLCs cultivate a culture of shared expertise and mutual support.

Mentorship is highlighted as a pivotal strategy for teacher development under NEP 2020. The policy advocates structured mentorship programs where experienced educators guide less-experienced colleagues. This personalized support helps teachers refine skills in areas such as classroom management, lesson planning, and student engagement. By providing constructive feedback and practical guidance, mentorship programs build confidence and competency, particularly for early-career teachers.

Pre-service teacher education also undergoes a significant overhaul under the policy. The Bachelor of Education (B.Ed.) program is extended to a four-year degree, integrating theoretical instruction with practical experience through internships and classroom observations. This comprehensive approach aims to better prepare aspiring teachers for the realities of the profession, equipping them with both academic foundations and hands-on skills.

Teacher recruitment and career advancement are addressed with an emphasis on merit and motivation. NEP 2020 calls for higher standards in teacher selection and merit-based promotions, ensuring that the most capable and dedicated individuals enter and thrive in the profession. By linking career progression to performance and contributions, the policy seeks to enhance the status and appeal of teaching as a career.

The policy also emphasizes recognizing and rewarding excellence in teaching. Schools and districts are encouraged to implement systems that celebrate exceptional teaching practices through awards, public recognition, and financial incentives. Such initiatives aim to foster a culture where teachers feel valued and inspired, reinforcing their commitment to professional growth and excellence.

11.7 Assessment Reforms: From Rote Learning to Competency-Based Evaluation

The National Education Policy (NEP) 2020 introduces a comprehensive overhaul of student assessment practices in India, aiming to move away from traditional reliance on rote memorization towards a competency-based framework. This reform seeks to create a more meaningful and holistic evaluation process that emphasizes critical thinking, creativity, and the application of knowledge, aligning assessments with the broader goals of student development.

A key component of NEP 2020 is reducing the dominance of high-stakes examinations, such as board exams, that have historically shaped the Indian education system. These exams, often focused on factual recall, have fostered a culture of rote learning, causing significant stress while failing to capture the breadth of students' abilities. The policy seeks to replace this approach with evaluations that measure a broader range of skills, encouraging learners to engage more deeply with subject matter and apply their understanding to practical problems.

Central to this shift is the adoption of Competency-Based Education (CBE), where assessments gauge students' mastery of specific skills and concepts. Unlike traditional tests that assess rote memorization, CBE focuses on the practical application of knowledge. For instance, a mathematics assessment might require students to apply a formula to solve a real-world problem, ensuring they understand its theoretical underpinnings and practical utility. This approach cultivates problem-solving and analytical skills, fostering a deeper engagement with learning.

Formative assessments, integral to NEP 2020, play a pivotal role in this transformation. These evaluations provide continuous feedback throughout the learning process, enabling teachers to monitor progress and identify areas where students require additional support. Unlike summative assessments, which occur at the conclusion of a course, formative assessments include tools such as quizzes, classroom discussions, and project-based activities. This ongoing feedback loop allows educators to tailor their instruction and implement timely interventions, ensuring students build a strong conceptual foundation before advancing.

The policy also emphasizes holistic assessment practices, which evaluate students across a range of domains beyond academics. This includes extracurricular involvement, leadership skills, teamwork, and social-emotional development, reflecting the NEP's commitment to nurturing well-rounded individuals. For example, contributions to community service or collaborative group projects might be considered in a student's overall evaluation, highlighting skills essential for success in both academic and real-world contexts.

The integration of technology further enhances the assessment process under NEP 2020. Digital platforms enable interactive, adaptive assessments that adjust question difficulty based on student performance, offering a nuanced measure of individual abilities. Immediate feedback provided by these tools helps students identify mistakes and refine their understanding in real-time. For educators, digital systems provide detailed analytics on student performance, enabling a data-driven approach to instruction and curriculum planning.

To alleviate the stress associated with traditional examination systems, NEP 2020 introduces greater flexibility in scheduling and structure. Modular exams, for instance, allow students to attempt assessments in smaller, spaced intervals rather than a single comprehensive test. This system supports continuous learning, reduces pressure, and provides students with multiple opportunities to demonstrate their competencies, creating a more supportive evaluation framework.

The policy also prioritizes competency-based assessments in foundational literacy and numeracy, recognizing these skills as critical for all future learning. Regular evaluations in early education are designed to monitor students' progress in reading, writing, and basic mathematics, ensuring these competencies are achieved by Grade 3. Early identification of learning gaps enables timely interventions, helping to establish a robust foundation for further academic success.

At the higher education level, NEP 2020 encourages reforms to align assessments with the goals of multidisciplinary learning and practical skill development. Universities and colleges are advised to adopt diverse evaluation methods, including traditional examinations, project-based assessments, internships, and research activities. This multifaceted approach provides a more comprehensive understanding of students' abilities, better preparing them for the complexities of the workforce.

11.8 Challenges and Opportunities for Implementing NEP 2020 in Indian Classrooms

The implementation of the National Education Policy (NEP) 2020 offers both significant challenges and promising opportunities for reshaping India's education landscape. While the policy envisions a modernized and holistic approach to learning, achieving its objectives requires meticulous planning, substantial resources, and collaboration across diverse educational stakeholders. To fully realize the potential of NEP 2020, it is crucial to address the challenges while leveraging the opportunities it presents.

Challenges:

One of the most profound challenges is the sheer diversity and scale of India's education system. With over 1.5 million schools serving millions of students from varied socio-economic, cultural, and linguistic backgrounds, ensuring that the reforms are uniformly implemented across all regions is daunting. Rural and underserved areas face additional barriers, including inadequate infrastructure, a dearth of qualified teachers, and limited access to digital tools. Bridging this urban-rural divide necessitates focused efforts to enhance infrastructure, provide equitable educational opportunities, and expand digital connectivity.

Teacher preparedness emerges as another critical challenge. NEP 2020 proposes a departure from traditional pedagogies toward methods like experiential learning, competency-based assessments, and integration of technology in classrooms. However, many educators, especially in rural areas, are more familiar with conventional teaching approaches. Comprehensive and continuous professional development programs will be essential to equip teachers with the skills and confidence required to adopt these innovative strategies effectively.

The digital infrastructure gap poses a significant hurdle to achieving the policy's emphasis on technology integration in education. Although NEP underscores the importance of digital learning tools, reliable internet access, computers, and technological resources remain scarce in numerous schools, particularly in remote areas. While initiatives such as Digital India aim to address these gaps, the scale of investment required to bring digital equity across the nation remains substantial.

The transition to competency-based assessments and holistic evaluation represents a cultural shift that challenges the entrenched exam-oriented mindset. For decades, high-stakes examinations emphasizing rote learning have dominated India's education system. Reorienting this culture to prioritize critical thinking, creativity, and real-world application of knowledge will require extensive re-education of educators, parents, and students. Schools must redesign assessment systems, introduce alternative evaluation frameworks, and build widespread awareness about the advantages of holistic learning approaches.

Opportunities:

Despite these challenges, NEP 2020 creates numerous avenues for transformative change. Among the most significant opportunities is the introduction of flexibility and choice in education. By enabling students to explore a wider array of disciplines, including vocational education, arts, and humanities, the policy promotes a multidisciplinary learning environment. This approach nurtures creativity, critical thinking, and problem-solving abilities, equipping students to excel in a dynamic global workforce.

The emphasis on experiential and skills-based learning offers another critical opportunity. Encouraging students to learn through real-world applications and hands-on experiences not only enhances engagement but also prepares them for practical challenges. Vocational training integrated into the school curriculum empowers students with industry-relevant skills from an early age, aligning their education with evolving economic demands.

Technology integration, despite its challenges, presents transformative potential for education delivery. Digital platforms and tools can democratize access to high-quality educational resources, bridging gaps between urban and rural learners. The establishment of virtual classrooms, digital libraries, and online learning forums ensures that students in remote areas receive the same quality of education as their urban counterparts. Moreover, personalized learning powered by artificial intelligence and adaptive technologies can address individual learning needs, enhancing both teaching and learning experiences.

FURTHER READING

1. **National Education Policy 2020** Ministry of Human Resource Development, Government of India. (2020).

[Available online: https://www.education.gov.in/en/nep-new]

2. **Educating the Whole Child: The Role of Social and Emotional Learning** Elias, M. J., & Zins, J. E. (Eds.). (2006). *Social and Emotional Learning in the Classroom: Promoting Mental Health and Academic Success.* Corwin Press. This book provides insights into the integration of social and emotional learning (SEL) in education, aligning with NEP 2020's emphasis on holistic development.

3. **Active Learning: Creating Excitement in the Classroom** Bonwell, C. C., & Eison, J. A. (1991). *Active Learning: Creating Excitement in the Classroom.* ASHE-ERIC Higher Education Reports. This report explores various active learning strategies, which are central to the pedagogical reforms discussed in NEP 2020 and the chapters on teaching methods.

4. **Educational Technology: A Theoretical Approach** Roblyer, M. D. (2006). *Integrating Educational Technology into Teaching.* Pearson Education. This book covers the effective integration of technology in classrooms, an area emphasized in NEP 2020 and the sections on technology-enhanced learning.

5. **The Flipped Classroom: Practice and Practices in Higher Education** Bergmann, J., & Sams, A. (2012). *Flip Your Classroom: Reach Every Student in Every Class Every Day.* International Society for Technology in Education. This text aligns with discussions on active learning strategies and the flipped classroom model in Indian education.

6. **Differentiated Instruction in Practice: A Resource Guide** Tomlinson, C. A. (2001). *How to Differentiate Instruction in Mixed-Ability Classrooms.* ASCD. A foundational book on differentiated instruction, relevant to the NEP's emphasis on catering to diverse learning needs in Indian classrooms.

7. **Inquiry-Based Learning and Teaching Across Disciplines** Justice, C., Rice, J., & Warry, W. (2009). *Inquiry-Based Learning: A Conceptual and Practical Resource for Educators.* Stylus Publishing. This book supports the discussions in the chapters on inquiry-based and discovery learning.

8. **Mindfulness and Education: Bringing Mindfulness Practices to Children and Adolescents** Rechtschaffen, D. (2014). *The Way of Mindful Education: Cultivating Well-Being in Teachers and Students.* W. W. Norton & Company. This book aligns with the chapter on mindfulness and emotional learning, offering practical insights for educators.

9. **Collaborative Learning Techniques: A Handbook for College Faculty** Barkley, E. F., Cross, K. P., & Major, C. H. (2014). *Collaborative Learning Techniques: A Handbook for College Faculty*. Wiley. This text supports the discussions on collaborative and cooperative learning techniques for Indian classrooms.

10. **Assessment for Learning: Principles, Policy, and Practice** Black, P., & Wiliam, D. (1998). *Inside the Black Box: Raising Standards Through Classroom Assessment*. Phi Delta Kappan. This work is essential for understanding competency-based assessments and the shift from rote learning, which is highlighted in NEP 2020.

11. **Educational Leadership and Reform** Fullan, M. (2007). *The New Meaning of Educational Change*. Teachers College Press. A key text for understanding the reforms in educational leadership, aligning with NEP 2020's goals for teacher training and professional development.

12. **Teaching in the 21st Century: Enhancing Learning Through Digital Tools** Koehler, M. J., & Mishra, P. (2009). *What Is Technological Pedagogical Content Knowledge?. Contemporary Issues in Technology and Teacher Education*. This journal article explains the integration of technology into pedagogy, which is central to NEP 2020's focus on digital learning.

13. **The Role of Vocational Education in Economic Development** UNESCO-UNEVOC International Centre for Technical and Vocational Education and Training. (2018). *Vocational Education and Training: Key to the Future*. This UNESCO report is aligned with the NEP 2020's emphasis on integrating vocational education from an early stage.

14. **The Art of Problem Solving in Education** Polya, G. (2004). *How to Solve It: A New Aspect of Mathematical Method*. Princeton University Press. Relevant to discussions on problem-based learning and critical thinking, this classic text provides insights into problem-solving methodologies.

15. **Innovations in Education: Lessons from Pioneering Schools** Zhao, Y. (2012). *World Class Learners: Educating Creative and Entrepreneurial Students*. Corwin Press. This book discusses the need for innovative teaching methods that encourage creativity and entrepreneurship, aligned with NEP 2020's vision for future-ready education.